A GRAIN OF MUSTARD SEED

Marcio Moreira Alves was a journalist in Rio de Janeiro at the time of the military take-over of Brazil in 1964. His articles against torture of political prisoners made him one of the few intellectual opponents of the regime and won him a seat in Congress in the 1966 parliamentary elections. His outspoken opposition on the floor of Congress to the generals' policies forced him into hiding in the underground of Brazil, and, in 1969, into exile from his own country. He has spoken throughout the United States on the current situation in Brazil. He now lives with his family in Paris.

A GRAIN OF MUSTARD SEED

The Awakening
of the Brazilian Revolution

by

MARCIO MOREIRA ALVES

Anchor Books
Doubleday Anchor Press
Garden City, New York
1973

The Anchor Books edition is the first
publication of A *Grain of Mustard Seed*

Anchor Books edition: 1973

ISBN: 0-385-00395-1
Library of Congress Catalog Card Number 72–84959
Copyright © 1973 by Marcio Moreira Alves
Printed in the United States of America

CONTENTS

To Those Who Will
Fall Along the Way

INTRODUCTION

The Brazilian Congress has a good survival record for Latin America: since independence, a hundred and fifty years ago, it has been closed five times and only for brief periods. The first time, in 1823, it defied Emperor Pedro I by voting a liberal constitution. Pedro showed his displeasure by having an artillery regiment surround Congress and send members home. Antonio Carlos de Andrada, Brazil's founding father, ceremoniously bowed, hat in hand, to "His Majesty the Cannon." The last time, on December 13, 1968, no troops were needed to enforce the government's will. Congress had voted to preserve the immunities of a member who had called for the boycott of the National Day's parade and for an "Operation Lysistrata" by the wives and sweethearts of officers who were shooting students on the streets, censoring political debate and throwing into prison workers who struck against a wage policy that reduced their buying power merely to survival levels. The ruling generals, playing on their colleagues' machismo, united the Armed Forces against the normally servile legislators. They had only to make a phone call to empty the twin-towered, double-domed building which Brasília's architect Oscar Niemayer had meant to symbolize the people's control over their government. Hatless contemporary congressmen had neither the will nor the leisure to indulge in symbolic protest.

I was the congressman who served as a pretext for the military to grab whatever portions of dictatorial power they had neglected to seize in 1964, when they took control of the country. Since then I had tried to denounce the choking of public and private liberties in Brazil through the press and, from 1966 on, through Congress. When both these instruments were silenced I went on, starting from the secret channels of clandestine networks, then using the broader possibilities of political havens abroad. This book, born in exile and published in several foreign languages, is the continuation of my work. It is both a description of my country's recent political history and social realities and of the motives that force so many of us, members of a privileged class in an unjust society, to rise and fight for our country's liberation.

In Brazil, in Latin America, in every colonized region of the underdeveloped world, rebellious members of the dominent classes are a spark that can fire revolution. Fidel Castro, heir to a landowning family; Ernesto Che Guevara, an upperclass doctor; Father Camilo Torres, an offspring of the Colombian oligarchy are exceptional in their accomplishments, not in their choice. In all our countries thousands of men and women forsake their privileges, risk their lives, and take up arms. They see revolution not only as a class struggle but also as the way of freeing their people from a system of international exploitation that will forever keep them poor and in bondage.

Tracing the slow progress of my own political awakening, I have tried in this book to reconstruct an experience that is daily repeated in my country and in my continent. I feel that if we understand this type of political evolution better we can more quickly build our liberation. Also, knowing that under present circumstances this book will not be openly published in Brazil, I had the foreign reader in mind. Even when sympathetic and knowledgeable, he is baffled by our politics and at a loss to explain them through traditional methods, Marxist analysis not excluded.

My description of events in which I took part, such as the closing down of Congress, the effort to stop torture through documentation of its practice, the growing radicalism of the political options of Christian groups are, I hope, aids to the understanding of the complexities of Brazilian life. The stories I tell about my family and the hinterlands from which it came are meant to provide a few insights to the violent rural society that survives in spite of polluted, impersonal industries of São Paulo and Rio de Janeiro.

The book is increasingly depersonalized as it moves from past to future, from the background of the 1964 military coup, to the establishment of a dictatorship that holds profits as its sole social goal, to the revolutionary movements that are its natural consequence. Personal stories, though they may be of interest to clarify an evolution, are of little importance to the long popular struggle that is a revolution. In Brazil the people's struggle is just beginning.

Marcio Moreira Alves

CHAPTER I

UNDERGROUND

Crowded around the radio in the kitchen of a suburban home in São Paulo, we listened to the Minister of Justice. It was close to midnight, December 13, 1968, a Friday. His high-pitched voice, heralded by the trumpet blasts that the propagandists of the Brazilian military dictatorship so favor, was putting an end to an awkward political period. "Confronted by mounting subversive activities that even spread to the parliamentary members of the governmental party, who were supposed to defend the revolution of March 1964, the Government of the Republic refused to betray its duties toward social peace and economic development. . . ." One by one the rules were spelled out. On our silent faces, among the half-eaten sandwiches and warm beer, fell the juridical jargon, killing what guarantees of political and human rights still existed in Brazil. Congress was shut down. Habeas corpus for political prisoners was rescinded. The military could rule by decree, arrest whom they pleased, abolish political rights and electoral posts. Their acts could not be examined by the courts.

Events—even when expected—cause a pang of surprise, when they pass from the imagined to the lived. Everyone had expected the military eventually to seize absolute power. Thus went the internal logic of the regime. Many of us had organized our lives accordingly, living as if the law of the land were already like that just announced by the Minister. Some had left their jobs, their families, had moved to other towns under assumed names, and had learned to wear the mask of a false identity which is the conspirator's life insurance. These precautions were necessary, since the police and military intelligence had been on the go for months. Ever since November, when they had received evidence that Carlos Marighela had led the holdup of an armored car, they had reintroduced torture as a means of extracting information from political prisoners. For these, urban guerrilla warfare was already a fact of daily life. For the rest of us, however, it was still only an abstraction, toward which we were moving as we helped our friends. We lived amid a population aware of nothing, ruled by laws which, though they suspended some constitutional guarantees, kept up the appearance of a democratic system. I had been accustomed to fighting in the open since I first entered a newsroom at eighteen. I was also heir to a two-century-old dominant class tradition, which looks on the police as a necessary evil for the defense of property but who are never to be involved in struggles for political power. For me, all this underground life was a new thing. I regarded it with the slight incredulity of a well-meaning aristocrat setting foot in a slum for the first time.

The reality that had finally come to pass held us under its spell. The talkative ventured comments such as: "They finally did it!" or "It's open war now." The others kept to "Sons of bitches!" and other ritual curses—which in Portuguese lack the Spanish flamboyance, sounding as curt as their English equivalents. We decided to leave. I couldn't stay in the house. It had been safe enough as long as the hunt for me was not yet on in earnest, but now it might be searched. According to one of the rules I was to memorize in the next few days, the biggest game was always to arrive at meetings last and leave first. So, once again making use of a privilege, I left first, in company with the young lawyer who was to hide me for a week. He was to be the sole link between my endless hours of waiting and the outside world, to which I would go back only for brief and meticulously planned moments.

A clandestine life imagined is very different from what you actually live through. This I was soon to discover. Before we were faced with it, my wife and I had decided not to leave Brazil, no matter what happened. We knew that if Congress refused to lift my parliamentary immunity, either it would shut down or I would find myself in permanent risk of physical assault. In any case a "normal" life would be impossible for a long time. During our long morning talks in bed, the only place and time we could find to talk in those frantic days, looking at the leaves of the gigantic rubber plant that seemed about to swallow our house in Brasília, we explored the possibilities of an underground life for me, while Marie would take care of the children in Rio. We already had some notions of police savagery, but we viewed the uncertainties of the future as a purely masculine affair, where men fought and women continued the routines of survival, just as had happened through the countless generations of warfare that were a part of my wife's memory of France. Strangely, I believed in this idealized vision of revolutionary preparations in an underdeveloped, colonized, violent country like Brazil. As is true of so many Brazilians, resistance to an occupier was only a reference in my background, not a concrete experience. The process of political radicalization I had been through since the military take-over four years before, had been largely intuitive, intellectual. It had not been achieved at the cost of suffering, or through the hardening humiliations that so often accompany revolutionary options for workers and peasants. On the contrary, it had given me a purpose in life—a gift one can never be thankful enough for—and the opportunity to fight from fairly secure positions: as a member of the press and from Congress. It entailed little risk and many personal rewards—so great in fact that I had to learn to watch myself as an outsider might in order to shun ego trips and avoid being sucked into the system.

To see yourself as others see you is an excellent exercise in humility. I find myself ridiculous some of the time, especially when holding forth about something: teaching, making a speech, or going through the ritual ballets of courting. Often I have such a strong awareness that I'm manipulating people—sometimes in a ludicrously obvious way—that it seems impossible that those I'm with will not sense it. They don't. This naïveté makes the temptation to manipulate almost irresistible. Possibly the reason we are so easily fooled is that our pride will not accept even the possibility that someone is fooling us. The sharper we think we are, the greater the sucker we may be.

Be that as it may, at that time I imagined that my underground work would be accomplished with no immediate risk to my family. I even thought it would be possible, every once in a while, to meet Marie at some friend's country house for a few days of lovemaking, reminiscence, and conversation. Our twelve years together had made her grow into such a permanent part of me that I couldn't dream of life without her, even if I sometimes felt attracted by other women. I felt there must always be a possibility of seeing her, and I couldn't imagine it otherwise.

My ideas on guerrilla warfare had more to do with medieval jousting than with the sordid facts its fighters learn to live with. It is very difficult to tear oneself away from conventional patterns of thought even in such a dehumanizing field as killing quickly and well. My knowledge of warfare stopped at the well-ordered—and obsolete—massacres of Europe and Korea, in which soldiers were always granted pauses in which to rest their nerves and to make love. I assumed this could work just as well in Brazil, except that the pauses would have to be arranged secretly—a proposition that seemed entirely possible to someone who then had scant respect for the repressive talents of a police force that was unacquainted with the ways of Brazil's upper class.

The facts of life and the sloppy organization of the revolutionary group with which I had contacts were soon to destroy this arrogant attitude. And, in the process, were probably to save my life. To join an underground revolutionary organization is a total break with the past. You become the astronaut depending on improbable help in his wounded spaceship, Cortez wrecking his ships on Aztec reefs, the Alpinist tackling the virgin glacier. The transformation is so deep that at first you are amazed it doesn't show on your face when you walk the streets. You wonder how all the people you pass don't detect the stranger in you, don't sense the life you are living so differently among them. Then you start wondering how they in turn can live a normal life, go on their common errands, think about their jobs, their food, their football teams, their families or their weekends, when your own world is already empty of all this. Most of all you wonder how they care so little about what absorbs you so fully: the problems of political struggle, the transformations the country is going through. For to go underground is to walk alone in the dark, guided only by a few beacons—a phone call, a password, a meeting place, a magazine held upside down by strangers into whose hands you entrust your life. It is constant dependence and an ever-renewed act of faith. While you no longer can rely on your family and your lifelong friends, you put yourself at the mercy of unknown people who become the masters of your survival and on whom you depend even for such simple things as food, information, and shelter. You become part of a mysterious family of wives, husbands, children whom you see for a night, living at addresses you don't know or try at once to forget. Names become abstractions, like the words of a foreign language, for your own name is an assumed one, and so are those of your friends.

A clandestine life means being forever on the watch and in fear. First there is the fear of being recognized. You are always afraid that a passer-by, a neighbor in a restaurant, anyone in the crowds you elbow may spot you. You wonder what would happen if you stumbled on an acquaintance. Would he gossip? Would he inform on you? How would you react if suddenly, on the street, your name was called? You become irritated by the mirror that every morning sends back your changeless features. The efforts you make to alter them— the glasses you adopt, the modified hairdo, the mustache that grows with unbearable slowness—affect your face very little. No matter what, that face goes on being damnably familiar. There is the fear of spies, of the police. Anyone can be a spy. Why is the ice cream man standing today before the house and not at the corner? That tall mulatto in a blue shirt has already walked by three times in half an hour. What can he be up to? And the street sweepers, the taxi drivers, the delivery boys, the lovers in the shade of the lamppost, what are they all doing, why are they spying? Where will the first blow come from? The routines of life become menacing, full of meanings, hiding a thousand traps.

Underground you are always alone. And you are always

waiting. In a crowd you are the only one who is set on a purpose that has nothing to do with the trivial haste of your companions, and you feel that this singleness of purpose casts a spotlight on you, as if suddenly your skin had turned blue or your ears had grown into antennae. The people you have dealings with only rub their humanity against you for specific reasons, for brief moments. Idle conversations become a thing of the past, and only then you realize how important they are, how words can occupy your emotional spaces and stir your mind. You must learn to be your own company, to find rest and responses in yourself and, most of all, to wait. Normally life, to a great extent, consists in waiting for periods of action. Only you don't feel these empty hours so much, for you fill them with motions that you are conditioned to consider useful—the rush for trains and buses to work and home, the moving from one appointment to another, the planning and paperwork for a meeting, the washing and dressing for a party or a date. It is only when you are uprooted from normality that you meet head-on the dimension of time—and you bend under its weight.

Most of your time is spent in a room, cut off from the life of the house, whose visitors must not even suspect you are there. Or in a small, empty apartment where the bell is a dreaded threat. For hours on end you stare at the walls, memorizing the cracks, following the shades of the paint that after a while look like animals, monsters, or the cartoon faces. Your powers of concentration flag and you read no more than a few pages of a book before changing to another one. Though time is bottomless you are always waiting for something to happen, for someone to knock, and this anxiety stretches time even further.

As I stepped out into the street, after hearing the radio message from the dictatorship, I knew nothing yet of the cramped existence I was so soon to slip into. I got into the Volkswagen, Brazil's anonymous car, thinking of the neighbors—workers, civil servants, clerks—who had preferred sleeping to hearing the Minister's announcement. New laws, new restraints on their freedom, an iron dictatorship forced on the country meant very little to them. Their lives would go on unchanged. The only freedom that might make sense to them would be the right to strike and to organize unions freely. These rights had been abolished long ago, in 1964, as the military began to implement an economic policy calling for overcapitalization of the dominant classes at the expense of wages. Having to accept this, they were now uninterested in the rest and refused to sacrifice their short sleep to listen to the government's arguments and threats. Then I remembered the euphoric congressmen, the tearful secretaries, the emotion I had seen the day before on the faces of the guards, drivers and doormen in Brasília, proud servants of a Congress that had finally, in the face of oppression, stood up and been counted. The unreality of it all dawned on me. For over a month the upper classes of Brazil, hypnotized, had watched the clash between the Executive and Congress. They spoke or thought of little else, followed the details through millions of printed words, learned to recognize the actors through hundreds of pictures and hours of television exposure, and waited with bated breath for the outcome. All this interest, all the drama didn't even touch the people's imagination. We had lived an entirely superficial crisis. Now, still a member of the superstructure, I was awake and moving to a hiding place; my colleagues were wondering about their future, most of them already repenting their moment of courage; the military were drawing up their purge lists and sending the police after their enemies—and the people were sleeping.

The brief period in which my own life coincided with the political life of Brazil closed at three o'clock on the afternoon of December 12, 1968, when three hundred congressmen broke into applause at their own temerity in ending long years of humiliation at the hands of the military. Men hardened by years of political swindling, with consciences blunted by unwavering service to power, wept and hugged each other. The women who sat in the predominantly masculine semicircle had black streaks running down their cheeks, and lipstick smeared all over their faces. Even some journalists, for whom losing their cool is a professional blunder, had tears in their eyes.

The Speaker announced the final vote: "One hundred

and forty one Honorable Members approve the proposition. Two hundred and sixteen Honorable Members reject it. There are twelve blank votes. The proposition is rejected." The end of the sentence was drowned out. In the guests' gallery someone started singing the national anthem. The bell rang calling for silence, but the song flowed on, louder as other voices joined in, gathering strength from word to word, from note to note. It overcame the bell and finally took possession of the whole building, forcing the Speaker and the other officials to stand to attention.

The miracle a small group of opposition members had so carefully planned had occurred: a hand-picked Congress, elected by fraud in the countryside and under every kind of intimidation in the cities, had rebelled. The military's two-thirds majority vanished when a hundred of its members crossed party lines to support the right of an unpopular congressman to speak his mind from the floor. After limply surrendering its most important attributes and privileges, after being purged, closed, and threatened, Congress had chosen to stand firm.

Backed by the President, helped by the bullying tactics of the Minister of Justice, the military ministers had asked Congress to strip me of my parliamentary immunity. In August and September, while violence against workers and students was becoming more frequent on the streets of the country's main cities, I had made a series of speeches against police brutality and torture of political prisoners—then already rampant. A few days after the storming of the University of Brasília—organized as a provocation by the chief of police, when students were herded from classes to be beaten while several were shot in the central square of the campus—I had called for the boycott of the Independence Day parade which, in Brazil, is the annual proof that the Army exists. In every town or even village where there are army barracks, the troops parade, often beefing up their numbers with schoolchildren, boy-scouts, even nurses and the personnel of the anti-yellow fever campaign. In the larger cities it is the one day in the year when all tanks and armored vehicles run. In Rio twenty thousand troops, commanded by generals who for once try to get their bellies into battle fatigues, present arms to the President and the diplomatic corps in front of the Ministry of War, while World War II planes spread colored smoke in the skies.

Independence Day is the symbolic, all-out manifestation of the military presence. It is also a justification for an army that lost its defensive function (there being no foreign wars) and it serves as a deadline for the drilling of conscripts. It is so important that the annual cycle of military life turns around it, the year starting from one and ending at the beginning of another.

My iconoclastic speech, concerning Independence Day, however, went further than maculating the magic day. I had also called for an Operation Lysistrata: the officers who in silence tolerated, and thus approved of, their colleagues' violence toward prisoners were to be boycotted by their wives and sweethearts. Operation Lysistrata was considered by the Armed Forces to be the ultimate offense. Here was this spoiled brat, scion of a long line of politicians who had always served the dominant classes well but who had somehow acquired what to them were dangerous Communist opinions, not only calling them a gang of torturers, but going to the groin and attacking their *machismo!* It was to be a provocation ideally suited to the plans of a group of officers who, in the growing upheaval of middle-class opinion, read the end of their sway. They realized that, for autocratic rule, even a little freedom is too much. Unconfident about the success of policies enacted by an Armed Forces Government, feeling unpopular to the point of no longer daring to walk the streets in uniform, afraid of having to answer for their acts of violence if a liberalized regime renewed the power of the courts, this group had been planning a total dictatorship ever since the student demonstrations of June and July. Though it had close links with several key commanders in the all-important "Vila Militar," the barracks compound outside Rio where most of Brazil's well-equipped units are stationed, they wanted to play it safe and rally the support of the military rank and file.

Some young officers, mostly captains and majors at the Escola de Aperfeicoamento de Oficiais, a training school that opens the way to further promotion, had been making nationalistic noises in opposition to the government's unabashedly pro-American concessions. Their democratic inclinations were rightly judged to be nil, but they had to be co-opted in the event of another coup. Otherwise they might get the idea of overthrowing the generals and running the country themselves. The anti-machismo part of my speech had served this purpose perfectly. As a body blow within the grasp of the least perceptive ensign, it was used to divert officers from more serious preoccupations with the future of the country and the uses of power. While they were ranting against me, against Congress, against the intellectuals and students, against the whole decadent set of probably homosexual institutions that made possible such an attack, while they were seeking ways of castrating me or taking some other exemplary revenge, they would not bother with the time-consuming exercises of political conspiracies. And, more important, they would probably support (as indeed they did) any measure aimed at chastening the offending power.

Almost unnoticed by the press, the speech was reprinted and circulated to all garrisons, including remote ones in the Amazon jungle.

Independence Day's parade went by normally, except in Goiânia, a city near Brasília, where the students infiltrated the marching lines and in no time had the parade pursuing them all over town, running and cursing in roaring disorder. I would like to think that the idea of Operation Lysistrata was also followed, but, of course, no one can ever produce evidence that it was. At any rate, the stage was set for the final maneuvers, which Queen Elizabeth unintentionally postponed.

Brazil is in some ways a surrealistic land. The actions of Brazilian high brass sometimes bewilder even us, the local natives. Generals have, for instance, the most extraordinary respect for the formal aspects of law. Not that they waver about doing something outrageously unlawful, but they always insist on hiring a jurist to set things straight after the fact. This is the reason why they give numbers to their transgressions of the Constitution, calling them "Institutional Acts," and do the same with constitutional laws, which are called "Complementary Acts" and are issued by the dozen.

It is as if they could not forget the long legalistic tradition of the Army, which had never been in power before 1964, and find it necessary to justify themselves through legal paraphernalia. They also worship protocol and precedence. When you speak to a general you have to adapt yourself to hierarchical jargon and understand, for instance, that when he says that so and so is more "modern" than he, he is not thinking of comparing their respective outlooks, but is only saying that the other one joined the Army later.

The protocol problems brought about by Queen Elizabeth's visit to Brazil in October 1968, upset the coup's timetable. It might, after all, seem unbecoming to disband Congress—where she was to be received—and start a major political crisis while the government was playing host to such a universal symbol of stability and lawful rule as British royalty.

So the confrontation was postponed, the Queen was feasted, the players had a break to array their troops for the final battle. For the opposition the truce was unprofitable, for we then had only faint clues about what was brewing among the hard-liners. My friends and I were unaware that my little speech had provided the pretext for a crisis, though I knew, from threats and curses that reached me through anonymous phone calls, that it had provoked strong reactions.

All my parliamentary activities had been one long, concerted provocation. A handful of congressmen, elected by the large cities where elections were free of the voting-booth control enforced in the interior, had decided to test to the limit the constitutional guarantees the military had left standing as a token to international—and especially American—liberal opinion. We fired off denunciations, launched congressional investigations, covered with our immunity all sorts of protest movements, mostly student demonstrations and worker strikes. Our connections with leftist movements were varied, but we shared a common hate for the regime and the justifying role it had assigned us.

We even indulged in what we called "cultural terrorism" against our fellow congressmen, for we were a proud, daredevil group. This consisted in taking turns at the floor debates to intervene in speeches when flattery of the regime or the military became too shameless. Brazilian parliamentary rules have it that a congressman may allow a colleague to break into his speech with a remark. It is considered bad form not to yield to these interruptions, a habit our unmannerly group put to maximum use. Most of the government supporters were tame notables from the interior—landowners, lawyers, doctors, merchants—whose function it was to bring from the federal government small benefits for their constituency, such as roads, schools, post offices, branches of the Bank of Brazil. Their learning, intellectual powers, and mastery of the language were no match for our wide-awake group of city-dwellers. Ingloriously easy, our verbal victories made the opposition steal most headlines and appear stronger than its numbers. It also made us highly unpopular in a Congress whose clublike work we messed up. Our colleagues regarded us much as a law-abiding tenant of a ghetto neighborhood looks upon a gang of juvenile delinquents—with impotent fear. We were named the "Immature Group," for every conservative body calls those who represent rebellious forces of change "immature," "hasty," "insane," "infantile," as if adjectives could stop time.

However ego-building and news-rich the "cultural terrorism" sport might be, I stopped practicing it after a few months. One day I had just hacked to bits with some biting remarks the speech of a São Paulo doctor and was sitting on my bench, feeling pleased with myself and reading a paper. The man came down from the rostrum and walked up to me. I thought he was going to let me have it (fist fights and even shootings are not unheard of in Brazil's Congress) and I instinctively braced up, getting ready to defend myself. But the man simply said, in his everyday voice, that he had paid four hundred dollars for someone to write the speech for him and that the money was lost. He no longer could mail it to his constituents, for it was ruined by my interruptions. He said that when he saw me near the microphone he knew I intended to wreck his speech and that is why he had been so reluctant to yield to me. My sense of fair play—hardly a virtue for politicians—was aroused. I apologized lamely. Though I continued to despise the little bastards who tried to make a career of kissing the military ass, I gave up this tactic.

The strategy behind our provocations was to strengthen the truly active opposition, especially the students, so that enough middle-class support could be whipped up and, with the help of some officers, sick by now of the Army's unpopularity and its anti-nationalistic policies, try to change the regime. The alternative for some, who had scant belief in a bloodless return to liberal democracy was the disruption of whatever liberal institutions survived. We already viewed the political outcome as a class struggle in which the military would not hesitate to use whatever violence they could muster. We felt an armed contest would eventually be forced on those who wanted to change Brazil's social structures. We knew that a ruling class such as ours, which monopolized such immense wealth and so many privileges, would not give them up without throwing at us every weapon it had.[1] Thinking it improbable that a significant part of the working classes would opt for underground struggle and armed resistance while there was still a chance for legal actions and open struggles, we felt the existing legal structures had to be exposed.

Violence is a choice one makes when there is no other. This is especially true of the oppressed masses, with their historical memory of massacres whenever they staged a rebellion. Therefore, we believed that only when it would become crystal clear to all that the system tolerated no dissent, that it would repress every bid for social justice or even for an elementary betterment of the masses' plight, would the possibility arise for organizing a revolutionary movement strong

[1] According to Celso Furtado (*Obstacles to Development in Latin America*, New York, Doubleday Anchor Books, 1970, p. 153) nine hundred thousand Brazilians have a per capita annual income of $6,500 or more, while 45 million live on less than $130 a year. Timothy King, an economist with the International Bank for Reconstruction and Development, states that "it has been estimated that the poorest 20% of income recipients received only 4.2% of total personal income and the richer 20% received 65%. The richest 1% received 28%." (Cf. Economic Department Working Paper No. 88, International Bank for Reconstruction and Development, October 13, 1970, mimeographed, p. 151.)

enough to represent an alternative to the present power structure. It followed that the legal façade the dictatorship had built, of which Congress was a part, had to be brought down. In this perspective we considered it our duty to bring about a confrontation from which the surviving liberal institutions either would emerge strengthened—a tactical victory— or would go down for good.

I had no idea, of course, that my Independence Day speech would serve this purpose. I had meant it just as a wild volley and assumed that the really effective artillery pounding was the long and documented speeches on torture, the detailed analysis of the control foreign interests were acquiring over the country's economy, indeed any of the dozens of themes our group had explored from the floor. These were rational attacks. But, as it became apparent, what the military were waiting for was something that would produce a gut reaction.

The first public move in the battle was the arrival, at the Supreme Court, of a petition signed by the ministers of the three military services calling for my court-martial for offenses against the Armed Forces. This document was sent on to the House where it went to the Justice Committee. Soon it became clear that, despite a nominal two-thirds majority, the government couldn't count on the affirmative vote of most of its jurists. To abolish freedom of speech from the floor was, for their juridical training and parliamentary pride, a price too dear to pay for federal favors. So, after a nononsense visit from the Minister of Justice, the civilian mouthpiece of the military hard-liners, the majority whip obediently changed the appointments of nine of the members of the committee. This was an unprecedented attack against the most important committee in the House and a breach of long-established procedures. It must be remembered that Brazil's Congress, being the privileged political tool of the oligarchy, had a 140-year-old tradition that had only briefly been broken. A barefaced interference with its procedures and autonomy enraged even the tame representatives from the hinterlands, who viewed it as a fresh, harsh and, most of all, needless assault on their rights. Their historical perspective was dim, but they had an instinctive group reaction and timidly showed disagreement with the whip's action by cheering their expelled colleagues.

On November 30 it became clear that the game was being played in earnest. The government reconvened Congress in order to force an immediate vote on the question of my court-martial instead of waiting through summer vacations until March. Only then did we sense—and we were only a few—that war was declared with all guns blasting.

All through these weeks my life had been in shreds. Since we came to Brasília, in March 1967, we had lived in a house by the lake, with no immediate neighbors. Like all the houses in the city, it turned its back to the street and opened onto a garden, where Marie tended roses and tried to coax into flowers the European seeds that friends had brought her from Paris. We had the tallest eucalyptus in town; we had a huge rubber plant on which I hung a deep-blue and orange hammock; and there were a few yellow acacias and two jaboticaba trees which produced the cherrylike black fruits that most of us swear grow only in Brazil and in paradise. During the six-month dry season we kept assorted watering devices working all day and managed to keep the lawn almost green. A wall only four feet tall surrounded the house, mainly to keep out snakes and other animals that preyed on the neighboring vacant lots. The children, as everywhere in Brasília, lived in age-tribes. Always dirty and barefoot, they would spring out of nowhere—the nine-year-old tribe or the dreaded seven-year-old one—and invade the house, thirty or forty strong, emptying it of anything edible, undaunted by cries and curses, spilling water everywhere, knocking over the furniture and then joyfully moving on to another house.

Charming as it was for family life, a house that could so easily be conquered by seven-year-olds was not ideal for defense. By then, defense had become one of our great worries, for I was constantly receiving threatening phone calls and one of our military informers came up with warnings that a group of young Air Force officers was planning to kidnap me and beat me up. This had happened to others, and I had no intention of suffering either the physical pain or the political loss of face that this sort of petty humiliation might represent. I started to carry a gun and would no longer go out alone. We had floodlights set in the garden and at least one armed guard in the house at all times. The day guard, an Amazon Indian who had been assigned to protect me by an underground group, had quite a terrifying face and a gun so big that it made him walk sidewise, but I soon found out that his shooting experience was no greater than mine. At any rate, he was a very pleasant fellow, a great help with the garden and the children, to whom he told stories of crocodiles and jaguars.

In no time the house bristled with guns. I even gave my wife a ladies' .38 that came in a jewelry case. Though I had made her practice with it, she was more afraid of possible harm to the children than of any attack on the house. She kept locking guns in drawers and cupboards, hiding the keys in other drawers and cupboards, and, for added security's sake, promptly forgetting where the keys were, so that at any given time, and in spite of my protests, at least half our firing power was unavailable.

When you are a law-abiding citizen fighting for a righteous cause, the fact that you can't trust the police and must tend to your own security comes as a shock. Strangely, your possible disregard for the political institutions reduces not a whit your expectation of protection from common criminals. When you are denied it, it is as if you fall back on ruder times, to a frontier post or medieval town, or as if you were down to living in a ghetto, where "order," as personified by policemen, is actually oppression.

In a ghetto you quickly get around to considering society an enemy. So did we, in our open fortress, and we even derived some pride from our alertness and what we thought were adequate preparations. Then a congressman from Pernambuco came on a visit. He demoralized us! Though he saw the guard's forbidding looks and the arsenal spread on the tables, he asked how I could be so thoughtless as not to protect myself.

Horizontal violence—the bloody struggles for power among clans of the dominant class—is an old tradition in Brazil. In the interior, in the poorer states where control of the local administrative machine means not only social status but prosperity, such disputes are still settled at gunpoint.

Political leaders have bodyguards, even private militias, and would never dream of walking about unarmed, be it only to the beach in Rio. Pernambuco, as all the other states in the northeastern poverty bowl, follows this tradition. My friend believed in it, despite his socialistic views. Taking his coat off and revealing a revolver that hung as naturally from his belt as a tie from his neck, he proceeded to show Marie and me how easily we could be encircled and murdered. With a commiserating look he called our weapons rubbish and made up a list of what we should acquire to be moderately safe: two light machine guns, five rifles, at least three thousand rounds of ammunition and no less than five experienced men to be kept permanently in the house. He then went on for an hour matter-of-factly describing gun fights and narrow escapes in his home state, as if these were experiences normal to everyone in politics.

"You see," he told me, "sometimes the hardest thing is not to defeat your enemy but to control your men. You know I'm a man of reason, a lawyer, someone non-violent" (which, in fact, I had thought him to be up to that day). "Well, once I was helping a friend run for mayor of Limoeiro, a town where my family has always had a say in politics. The governor named a chief of police against us. The man started harassing my friends—beating them up, arresting them, sending cattle into their crops, that sort of thing. He even threatened me and was rude to some of my relatives. I either had to protect myself or lose face. If I let the man go I would be run out of town. So I was forced to arm a few men in the house with the sort of trustful hardware I just told you to buy. My father borrowed a bodyguard from a friend in Alagoas, a well-known and respected professional. His presence in town was enough to sober the chief of police, and this was all I wanted. I really didn't want to kill or harm the man. This was a tough idea to put into the head of the bodyguard. He couldn't understand that I wouldn't want to kill someone who might want to kill me or my friends. But I gave him strict orders to lay off and though I knew he felt frustrated and probably looked on me as some kind of a queer, things went well for a time. One day the bodyguard came and told me that he had been tailing the policeman. The man visited his mistress on the other side of the river every night. 'You know, doctor,' the bodyguard said, 'right near the bridge there's a big rock. God put it there. From behind that rock even a blind man could send this policeman to hell. If God didn't want this He wouldn't put the rock there. And we shouldn't disobey God's will.' I got real mad and told the bodyguard I would let him go to jail if he shot the policeman. Do you know what he did? There was a big lamp right above the police station's front door. Well, one day he cut the chain with a rifle shot and dropped the lamp on the head of the policeman. As he had disobeyed me, I gave him a good scolding and sent him back to Alagoas. But it was a good thing after all. Next morning the policeman left town."

After hearing this, my wife and I decided not to push things too far (Marie was particularly distressed at the prospect of feeding four extra men) and to leave things as they were, insufficient as our defenses might appear to professional eyes.

In Minas Geraes, a state renowned for the practical wisdom of its politicians, people say that what matters in politics are not the facts, but the versions. I daresay this applies also to other matters. It became known that I carried a gun and had a home full of weapons. Through no personal effort of mine I had gained the reputation of being able to use them, for I had been a correspondent in the Suez Canal Zone in '57 and was machine-gunned in Alagoas while covering a political dispute. Having once been a target, I was assumed capable of marksmanship. Reputations are made of twisted logic and half-baked truths one can never set straight, even with effort. But inaccuracy can be rewarding, as I found out, and in this as in other matters I learned to be careful about not telling all I knew about myself. The threats were not carried out. Perhaps, as a pawn in a general plan, I was more useful in one free-moving piece than as a cripple or a corpse. Or else I was spared simply because Brazilian officers stand in awe of bullets and gunpowder and wouldn't take lightly the idea of facing both.

The unwarlike spirit of Brazil's armed forces is not easy to imagine for anyone unfamiliar with Brazilian history. Brazil sent only one division to Europe, made up mostly of conscripts, during World War II. Since then the Army has never fought. Its four interventions in the political life of the country[2] were all bloodless and decided by telephone. In each case the side with more tanks and artillery won the day, without firing a shot. It was said that revolutions in Brazil were won by those who fell behind in their preparations to escape. Young officers never hear gunfire outside a practice range, but they cultivate bureaucratic heroics and their speeches are full of verbal explosions. And they strongly tend to overreact when they feel threatened—not only by political maneuvers, as we were soon to see—but also by physical danger. Whenever they must face a student demonstration or arrest a subversive, the display of force is so disproportionate to the threat that one wonders if it is so through fear or a desire for overtime pay.

Having thus far survived the growing crisis, I arrived at its climactic day in December determined to make this a habit. I knew Congress would uphold my immunity, for our little planning group, now helped by a few older and experienced congressmen, had closely followed the voting trends. At first we only marked on our lists the votes of the majority's jurists. Then we started to mark those congressmen whose privileges kept them immune from prosecution for common crimes. In Brazil parliamentary immunity had always been broadly interpreted to protect congressmen from every sort of judicial prosecutions. Among our colleagues there were some twenty accused of various crimes, from murder to fraudulent bankruptcy. One, a man from Alagoas, was said to have thirty-two marks on his gun. They would not risk voting for a precedent on a political crime that could blast their own parliamentary protection which, in some cases, they had bought dearly.

After noting down these congressmen, we started to notice more serious goings-on. The ministers of Foreign Affairs and of Labor, ambitious politicians with little backing in

---

[2] The ousting of Getúlio Vargas, in 1945; a preventive coup to secure President-elect Juscelino Kubitschek's inauguration in 1955; the movement in favor of the constitutional succession of resigning President Jânio Quadros by Vice-President João Goulart, in 1961; and the military take-over of 1964.

the barracks, told their congressmen friends to vote against the government. They each wanted to run for President, a post filled by the vote of parliamentarians ever since the 1967 Constitution, and only stood a chance if Congress freed itself from military pressure. Old generals of the Castelo Branco[3] group, who were at odds with Costa e Silva's followers, began counseling their friends to do likewise, hoping that one of them would grab power in the ensuing scramble. Finally Carlos Lacerda, the country's most talented right-wing politician, who had grown disenchanted with the military when they refused to hand him the presidency, produced a few colonel friends from his conspiratorial vintages. They told members of the majority that if Congress would not fend for itself, it would become so feeble that the military needn't send troops to shut it down—telling the doorman to do so would be enough.

If I had no doubts about the outcome of the congressional vote, I wasn't at all sure about its consequences. I knew only two things: that the political balance would change radically and that I stood a good chance of being murdered. This latter prospect struck me as unpalatable. Moreover, I intended to stay around in case a fight broke out among the military groups. We thought that if this happened one of the groups—probably the weakest—would follow the Dominican Republic model and hand out arms to the people. Once this was done, be it only on a small scale in a single big city, the military would either have to change the nature of the struggle, infusing it with social connotations, or they would lose control. In either case the very core of Brazil's political life would be changed.

Wishful thinking, added to a normal attachment to one's skin, can work wonders. I entered Congress on that morning of December 13 fully prepared to make myself scarce as soon as the whole business was over. This calmed my nerves and gave me a strange aloofness. Since what was the main drama for almost all present was only an anticlimax

[3] Marshal Humberto Castelo Branco was Brazil's first military dictator, from 1964 to 1967. He was succeeded by his Army Minister, Marshal Costa e Silva, who died in 1969. His successor was Marshal Emilio Garrastazu Medici, whose term ends in 1974.

for me, I was less involved and therefore could perform more effectively.

It is said that a good speech may change views but cannot alter votes. I built mine in a way I thought best not to lose votes, keeping at the same time to my highly unpopular principles of social justice and anti-militarism. Once I had delivered it and seen, with pleasure, that the results were excellent, I went to the minority leader's office to listen to the vote count through the microphones. We gathered there, my wife, my anxious parents, a few friends and journalists. As the government's defeat developed, I felt more and more detached. The room was erupting in tears, cries, embraces, while I was slowly coiling up into myself, as if I had nothing to do with what was happening. I kissed Marie, my mother, my sister, and did it once again for the photographers. I barely survived the loving bear-hug of my secretary. Then I handed to the newsmen a prepared statement calling for the re-establishment in Brazil of democracy and slowly, through a forest of outstretched hands and smiling faces, moved toward the rear exit of the House, where I had arranged for trusty friends to whisk me away. My fellow congressmen, many of whom had never spoken to the kamikaze hothead they saw in me, were like excited teen-agers mobbing the Beatles. Through me they wanted to embrace their own courage for having at last reacted against the military masters who so often had humiliated them. I moved on undisturbed, except when I fell into the arms of two or three of my closer friends. I remember whispering a warning into the ear of David Lerer, later to be the only congressman to be beaten up in jail for being not merely a "dirty Communist" but a "dirty Jew."[4]

[4] There is an undefined anti-Semitic trend among young Brazilian officers, especially those directly connected with repression. This is a disturbing development in a country that up to now has been spared this sort of problem. The signs are fuzzy, but already noticeable. Luiz Edgar de Andrade, a journalist who in 1969 was arrested and tortured by mistake, tells of swastikas at the headquarters of "Operação Bandeirantes," the main torture center in São Paulo, and of a weird conversation with his questioners—lieutenants and captains—who kept asking him if Hitler wasn't right after all. According to fellow prisoners, Chael Schreier, a twenty-three-year-old student, was tortured to death in Rio for being a Jew.

As I moved across the floor, followed by a group of colleagues, my main worry was to protect my right hip, from which a gun hung awkwardly. Now I felt ashamed of being armed and didn't want others to notice it. This shame was the strangest reaction I felt, for not only must many other congressmen also have been armed but I had made no effort during the previous days to pretend I hadn't joined their numbers. We finally got to the hall. As we started down the long tunnel that leads to the library the first notes of the national anthem came over the loudspeakers. We stopped for a moment, hearing the struggle of the song against the Speaker's disciplinary bell. We moved on as the anthem won out. A journalist who I knew worked for the secret police asked me where I was going. I told him I would go and rest at Cabo Frio, fishing and beachcombing. A few days later this tip got an old friend of my father's into jail. He had been Kubitschek's secretary but was already exclusively dedicated to securing his daily ration of scotch. A full Marine squadron came chopping down on the beach of the summer resort, in their best Vietnam manner, looking for me. As I was nowhere to be found, they arrested the only suspect of political connections in sight, giving the poor man a case of DT's.

My friends were faithfully waiting at the library's entrance. As I embraced my last colleague I thought, "If they don't get me now, I'll be safe forever."

My father and I got into the official car. We ran for a few miles; then I switched to a less obvious Volkswagen. Four years of public life, which had taken me from bourgeois liberalism to a profound revolutionary commitment, were then ending. I wasn't even tempted to look back at the Congress building, whose twin towers dominate Brasília and its plain of red earth. I had done my job as best I could. The hide-and-seek game of survival with the military was about to begin.

CHAPTER II

THE END OF GOULART

Blood is thicker than water. It was surely someone from the underdeveloped world who invented this maxim. Families, in our countries, have little in common with the vertical, self-contained organizations to which affluent societies have reduced them. They are clans. They provide general protection and social security—which the state, weak and insufficiently organized, is unable to do. When the clan is split by migrations, protection is taken over by the immediate community where one lives. It is quite common in the *favelas* for already large and needy families to take on one or two more children whose parents have died or disappeared.

In Brazil the bonds of kinship are stronger than those of political or religious affiliation. This strength shows even in the midst of ideological struggles. All sectors of society were shocked by the colonel who wrote his imprisoned and tortured daughter that a subversive could no longer be considered a member of the family; for his attitude attacked society's most intimate defenses. On the other hand, even the fiercest hardliners have grudging understanding of conservative parents who stand by their persecuted children or are politically influenced by them. In 1964 General Taurino de Rezende, head of the National Commission of Investigations, a post with powers similar to those of a chief inquisitor in sixteenth-century Spain, resigned and publicly denounced the repressive methods of his colleagues when his son, Sergio, a teacher at the University of Pernambuco, was arrested and beaten up for professing "subversive" opinions. My own father, while secretary of finance for the state of Guanabara, a key post in the economic administration of the country, was never bothered, despite my notorious anti-dictatorship activity. Only when he protested the police brutality against Rio's students was he made to resign, but even then he was never arrested or badly harassed. In 1970 a persistent rumor in Rio had it that Marshal Henrique Lott,[1] whose grandson, Nelson, had been arrested and tortured at the military police barracks, had shot to death the officer responsible for the tortures, one Major Fontenele. Considering that this man, known and dreaded, had rather suddenly vanished, the story was held for true. No one was surprised that Lott was free and tending his garden at a mountain resort. In a country where the press is censored, rumors spread like wildfire. This one became so entrenched, that the government had the old marshal interviewed on TV to deny having killed anyone.

In Brazil a relative is a relative, no matter what he has done, he must be helped if in need. This is a rule that holds even today, when the military are known to torture suppliers of "logistic" support (shelter, money, transportation) to revolutionaries as much as they torture the revolutionaries themselves. In 1964, when Brazil was still ignorant of what a truly repressive regime is, it was even stronger.

On April 10, 1964, ten days after the putsch, I published an article assailing the suppression of certain constitutional guarantees—in particular, the right of the accused to a public defense—included in the "Institutional Act of No. 1." My liberal sympathies and legal training were shocked by what I then considered the most arbitrary law ever enacted in the history of Brazil. I was also especially put out by the junta's choice of an author for this law: Dr. Francisco Campos, an ex-Fascist, a cynical and brilliant maverick jurist. This was the man who had written Brazil's 1937 dictatorial constitution. My class in law school had been taught to regard him as the archetype of the dishonest lawyer, who hires out his

[1] Marshal Henrique Teixeira Lott was Minister for War from 1954 to 1960. He led the preventive military coup that made possible President-elect Juscelino Kubitschek's inauguration in 1955. A presidential candidate in 1960, he was defeated by Jânio Quadros. In 1965, during a two-week attempt to run for governor of Guanabara, he published strong criticism of the regime. His candidacy was stopped by a legal technicality.

brains to the highest bidder. At that time most of us had a divided reaction to Getúlio Vargas.[2] We admired his nationalism but rejected his personalistic rule and early admiration for the Axis. Our judgment, based on moral grounds, reflected the general attitude of Brazil's middle classes. I felt that the rediscovery of Vargas' Minister of Justice by this new government, officially established in the name of morality and democracy, to carry out the same old liberticidal tasks, was a provocation and an evil omen.

The protest I wrote was a criticism by an insider. On the whole I favored the military coup. There was an urgent need, I felt, for basic reforms, especially for the redistribution of land, for wider educational opportunities, for nationalistic economic policies and, in general, for more social justice. But I felt this in an intuitive way, for humanitarian and idealistic reasons. My college-day Marxist readings had receded to a forgotten corner of my mind. They had not converted me—though I later realized Marxism had shaped my social analysis more than I then knew.

During the fifties Marxist studies were something of an academic status symbol. They were unofficially promoted by groups of Communist students who scouted freshmen they thought showed promise. Study circles were formed with these students, at first around the legal questions we were all studying, then shading off into Brazilian problems as a whole. Then as now it was impossible to avoid the questions of imperialism when dealing with our realities. From developing a consciousness about economic dependence and

[2] An exceptionally astute politician, Getúlio Vargas headed the middle-class revolution of 1930. He was dictator from 1930 to 1945 and constitutional president from 1950 to 1954. His nationalistic policies threatened many powerful economic interests. Cornered by his enemies through a palace scandal, he took his life in 1954. He was the dominant Brazilian politician of the twentieth century and his influence is still felt today. For information on Vargas as well as the whole Brazilian political scene of the last forty years the best work is Thomas Skidmore, *Politics in Brazil: 1930–1964*, Oxford University Press, New York, 1967. A biography in English is John W. F. Dulles, *Vargas of Brazil*, University of Texas Press, Austin, 1967—a book whose extensive documentation is marred by a shallow analysis. A brief but, on the whole, satisfactory history of Brazil is *The History of Brazil*, New York, Columbia University Press, 1970.

exploitation to a systematic study of Marxism, the leap was short. Invitations to these study groups were highly prized, for they were known to include some of the school's most brilliant students. I joined one and stayed long enough to do some readings and acquire basic notions. Then I drifted away, absorbed by my work as a reporter, my growing family, and perhaps the pretty girls who at the time provided some of my strongest interests. I had no real quarrel with the society I lived in: it was treating me very well indeed, as I rather expected it to do. I didn't then see what a rotten lot this same society imposed on the overwhelming majority of my countrymen. The struggle against injustice starts when one awakens to it. I may have lacked in those days not only lucidity but also courage; though perhaps I can say that my selfishness was a subconscious and unrationalized escape.

What made me think that Goulart's ousting might not be such a bad idea was his inability to follow a program, to stand by his ministers, to rule. He seemed to be opportunistic, erratic and politically dishonest. He was weak and plainly unfit for the presidency of a nation in crisis that cried out for a strong-minded reformer. Some minor personal traits also helped stain Goulart's image: he was seen drunk in public, he let corrupt cronies maneuver him who were capable of sabotaging important reform policies when offered the right price, and he had a gaucho's penchant for whoring. Moreover João Goulart was a prey to deeper contradictions, such as increasing his landholdings while preaching agrarian reform. In short, the man was utterly disordered. Not even his closest aides and allies trusted him, and this attitude was widely shared by the upper and middle classes.

My revulsion to Goulart's type of leadership was more than just moralistic. It was also an instinctive political judgment. In Brazil, as in any other country in Latin America, the reshaping of society toward justice will demand austerity and hardship. Merely to feed the hungry—to speak only of a low-level biological need—the present consumer society, transplanted to our countries for the good of a few, will have to be destroyed. The privileged—a word that covers even workers in a land where stable employment is rare—will have to shed long-established habits. Sacrifices, self-restraint, discipline, will have to be imposed. The country's leaders must set the example. With his pals, land deals, and women, Goulart was the reverse of this sort of necessarily austere leader. He obviously enjoyed the trappings of power too much really to love it, for power is an absolute and demanding master that stands for no rivals. Material goods were what he thrived on, not ideas. Most people sensed this, and it ruined his credibility. Therefore, a short-lived military intervention to sweep him from office was not disagreeable to large segments of the country's middle classes.

Unlike so many of the Spanish-speaking countries around her, Brazil had never once experienced a military dictatorship. The Army was widely held to be politically unambitious, democratic and nationalistic.[3] Its previous interventions in the country's political life had been both short and bloodless. Power had always been handed back to the civilians. The Army—and the military in general—were thought largely to favor liberal-democratic institutions. Military speeches abounded in references to this basic allegiance, which their record seemed to support. Sometimes they went so far as to stress the uniqueness in Latin America, of this legalistic mentality of theirs, in contrast to the political greed of the Argentines and Venezuelans. A ruthless, irremovable military dictatorship seemed a far-fetched prospect to most Brazilians. In 150 years of our history this had never happened.

True, rightist and leftist politicians had been in the habit of accusing one another's side of conspiracy and of knocking at the barracks' doors, but these accusations seemed to spring rather from rhetorical needs than from genuine fears. Among the prolific writings of left-wing intellectuals of the sixties, only one book—Wanderley Guilherme's *Quem*

---

[3] For the stereotypes commonly held by civilians about the military in Brazil, J. J. Johnson, *The Military and Society in Latin America*, Stanford University Press, 1968, is a good guide. The author shared these misconceptions and fell victim to them. Written along similar lines and plagued by the same false assumptions is Edwin Lienwen, *Arms and Politics in Latin America*, New York, Frederick A. Praeger, 1967. A Brazilian view is found in Nelson Werneck Sodré, *Historia Militar do Brasil*, Rio de Janeiro, ed. Civilização Brasileira, 2nd edition, 1968.

Dará o Golpe no Brazil? (Who Will Carry out the Coup d'État in Brazil?)—predicted a right-wing dictatorship ushered in by the Army. Guilherme's prophetic warnings fell on deaf ears. They were regarded as unrealistic even by the Communist Party leadership, who made caution a point of survival. No wonder that when the generals moved in, the left was caught napping and the liberal middle classes sided with the generals. While Goulart and his followers scrambled for safety, abandoning the few who, like ex-Education Minister Darcy Ribeiro, wanted to fight, the military maneuvered in a political vacuum and marched unopposed to power.

My denunciation of Institutional Act No. 1 was published on April 10, 1964 in the *Correio da Manhã*, Rio's liberal newspaper, on which I had started as a cub reporter and to which I was returning after two years of different pursuits. By breaking the press's unanimity in favor of the coup, my denunciation created an immediate political problem for the military, who were forced quickly to formulate a policy regarding press freedom.

The leaders of the coup had won widespread support among their military colleagues via two main arguments: they were going to re-establish discipline and respect for rank in the Armed Forces and to reinstate the constitutional democracy thought to be imperiled by João Goulart's social reforms and lust for personal power.

History's interpreters are often brainier than its actors. This, unfortunately, may lead them into error. Most students of the recent Brazilian political scene see the country's evolution through an abstract model governed by the general laws of class struggle and economic imperialism. Their theoretical interpretations take little account of history's accidents—highly regarded, by the way, by both Marx and Lenin—or of such secondary contradictions as the tensions created by military discipline. Therefore, though empirical data and even the plain testimony of the conspirators[4] stress its impor-

[4] Mainly General Costa e Silva's retrospective speech to the General Staff school students, published in *Jornal do Brasil*, April 1, 1965, General Olympio Mourão Filho's recollections, published in

tance, the problems of military unrest were downgraded by most analysts. The only one who gives it its proper importance is, unsurprisingly, a conservative: Fernando Pedreira,[5] a political reporter for a São Paulo paper involved up to its neck in the conspiracy.

Officers' reaction against the frequent breaches of discipline tolerated by Goulart, and his attempt to form with sergeants and petty officers a progressive military base to counterbalance the conservative generals and admirals were probably the most decisive factors for the coup's success. They furnished the conspirators with a large area of unanimity, centering around professional issues. Such unanimity could never have been welded around political opinions alone.

Brazilian law is hard on soldiers, sailors, and noncommissioned officers. They are allowed neither to vote nor hold office. In a military establishment which is never engaged in warfare their chances of rising through the ranks are dim. In the Navy, where full-time professionalism exists at all levels, as opposed to the Army's conscripts, a man's whole life hangs on his superior's whims. Even marriage is only possible with a hard-to-get special permission. The right to organize is limited to social activities. All these discriminations caused, during the late fifties and early sixties, political stirrings among the lower ranks of the military. In 1962 a few sergeants, taking advantage of legal loopholes, got themselves elected to Congress. Only one, a federal deputy from Rio, was actually inaugurated. When in 1963 the Supreme Court invalidated his election, his comrades rose in Brasília and, during one morning, held the nation's capital. This event became the starting point for more unrest and, conversely, a source of outrage for conservative officers.

In March 1964, during Holy Week, the Navy's lower ranks rebelled in Rio. Thousands of sailors and petty officers jumped ship and massed in the Metal Workers Union building. Their demands were simple: the right to organize, to

---

O *Estado de São Paulo*, April 2, 1965, and the journalistic description of the coup in Alberto Dines et al. in *Os Idos de Março*, Rio de Janeiro, José Alvaro, ed., 1964.

[5] In *Março 31*, Rio de Janeiro, José Alvaro, ed., 1964.

marry, to obtain better food and better pay. This meeting touched off visions of the Potemkin mutiny in the officer corps, the most elite in the Armed Forces. When the Marines sent to eject the sailors rallied to their cause, the naval officers in their panic demanded that the sailors' meeting hall be blasted by army tanks. Goulart turned this down. The decision he did take was typical of his vacillating leadership: after long-drawn-out negotiations he allowed the officers to arrest the sailors; he then immediately proclaimed an amnesty. The Navy Minister resigned and no other admiral would replace him. The government had to fall back on a retired officer whose relations with the Admiralty were strained, owing to his marriage to a black. The new minister proved unable to find officers who would serve on his staff. In the ships officers kept machine guns in their quarters and took turns to guard them from the sailors. The chain of command was broken.

The sailors' demonstration followed a huge meeting, held before the Army Ministry, during which Goulart launched a campaign to pressure the conservative Congress in favor of social reforms. Tanks guarded the square, where members of the outlawed Communist Party displayed banners calling for the recognition of their organization. Representing the newly formed General Confederation of Laborers, the head of the longshoremen's union, an old Communist hand, stood by the President. All the nation's progressive and Socialist politicians were present. They began what looked like a contest in revolutionary rhetoric. There was no relation between their language and the actual awareness of the masses. It was obvious that the meeting went a step toward a showdown with the country's reactionary forces and that the people were unprepared for such a test. Goulart led the battle with self-destructive haste. Helped by floods of scotch and the presence of his brother-in-law, Leonel Brizola, with whom he was fighting for the control of the Labor Party, he delivered a fiery speech, threatening with force those who stood in the way of a total transformation of Brazil's society. The high spot of the evening was the signing of several decrees empowering the government to expropriate land along federal highways, railroads, and dams, and nationalizing privately owned oil refineries. This was done under the glare of TV cameras; the whole country saw it. It scared the upper and middle classes as much as did the speeches. It meant Goulart was moving from words to acts. He had to be stopped then—or never.

Landowners, industrialists, conservative politicians, managers of American firms, the whole power complex of Brazil started to move fast. To build up public support for Goulart's overthrow, they planned and financed large demonstrations, most spectacular of which were the "Marches of the Family, with God, for Democracy." The one held on the eve of the coup put several hundred thousand people in the streets of São Paulo. On the military front contacts with the American embassy increased, and were maintained by General Cordeiro de Farias through the military attaché, General Vernon Walters, now second in command at the CIA, a friend since World War II of most of the conservative generals. The plotters wanted to enlist American support in case of civil war and make sure that their recognition as a legitimate belligerent would entitle them to military aid. Emissaries were sent to garrisons all over the country. In no time the conspiracy took shape. Only a last catalyst was needed to overcome the last legalistic misgivings of the army officer corps.

The catalyst was the sailors' uprising, reinforced by Goulart's last speech, which was delivered on March 30, 1964, to an assembly of sergeants and petty officers. This speech restated in stronger terms the ideas set forth at the meeting of March 13. It also warned the country of the impending reactionary plot and of the President's resolve to put it down. Broadcast by a nationwide radio and TV hookup, it helped convince the still wavering officers that the die was cast and that they must choose sides. They felt a direct menace. In 1952 a Populist revolution had disbanded Bolivia's Army, forming a popular militia and replacing most career officers by peasant and miner leaders. The officers thought that the sergeants' new political importance threatened their professional and social position and they believed that Bolivia's experience could serve as a model for Brazil.

On March 31, a small garrison went into open rebellion

in Juiz de Fora, a city halfway between Rio and Belo Horizonte. When the government troops sent to fight it rallied to the rebellion, the government's forces started to crumble, one by one, without a shot being fired. Finally General Kruel, commander of São Paulo and one of Goulart's closest friends, threw in with the rebels and the rout was completed.

Following this quick and effortless victory, the conspirators paused to form their hierarchy, work out their policies, select a leader. To avoid imperiling their victory by stirring unnecessary opposition, they soft-pedaled the initial purges in the Armed Forces. They had also to observe the niceties of legal rule, one of their main promises. Accordingly they sought the help of jurists, who adorned Institutional Act No. 1 with a pompous introduction, and called on Congress to ratify General Castelo Branco as the military's choice for President.

The decision to respect the freedom of the press was taken in line with these early self-imposed limitations. For the military this represented a calculated risk. In a land where half the population cannot read, the politically significant mass media are radio and TV. These had always been under censorship of sorts on the ground that they were public services and that the government must defend public morality. The new regime had only to tighten existing rules to achieve total control of the spoken word. As for the written word, it influenced only the classes upholding the coup, plus a small elite of urban workers.

There are no national newspapers in Brazil. The largest circulations do not exceed 250,000 copies a day, with a readership confined to each large city and its suburbs. Newspapers are mostly conservative, stanch defenders of the social status quo, free enterprise, and the principle of uncontrolled foreign investment in Brazil. Only two newspapers were critical of the military intervention. Both were published in Rio and one, the pro-Goulart *Ultima Hora*, was hampered in its action through involvement in financial scandals. Its owner had fled to Europe, where he awaited a chance to offer his services to the country's new masters. This left only the old liberal battlehorse, the *Correio da Manhã*, a paper with a long history of political activism, as the sole outspoken opponent of the anti-democratic measures taken by the government. For several months, until it was joined by the *Tribuna da Imprensa*, also a Rio daily, it became the only platform from which the liberals and nationalists among Brazil's intellectuals could voice their disapproval and anxiety to a Rio middle-class public. Alone in its courage, the paper found its audience spreading to other major cities. What copies trickled daily to Brasília, Porto Alegre, and even the state of Amazon's capital, Manaus, were sold on the black market. People gladly paid ten times the regular price and bribed newsboys to save them a copy. Often it was only through the *Correio da Manhã* that people learned of events in their home towns, whose papers either were afraid to displease local military authorities or upheld the government to the point of suppressing derogatory information. This was especially true of Recife's torture stories, which were seldom published locally.

My article against Institutional Act No. 1 moved the military, as it later leaked out, to abstain from imposing censorship. But their decision on this point remained for some time secret.

Right after the coup a witch-hunt started all over Brazil and the intellectuals became—as usual—a prime target. Brazil's repressive system was in a state of chaos. Yesterday's masters were on the run and the people they had the police watching were now loosing the same police on *them*. No one knew for certain from whom to take orders.

A blast of criticism amid such a superheated atmosphere could be risky for its author. Indeed the morning my newspaper article came out, my father called up suggesting I make myself scarce around Brasília. From his knowledge of national politics and previous coups he argued that the first days of a new government are the most dangerous. A responsible command does not yet exist and the rules for persecuting political foes are still to be laid down. Everyone stands at the mercy of violence. This being the situation, he said, there was no point in waiting for a possible blow from Vargas' ex-minister. To allow oneself to be arrested is foolish anyway—unless for a precise purpose such as a nonviolent protest—and so I decided to leave.

An underground network was already functioning to get people out of Brasília. I had learned of its existence a few days before from a congressman, who, though he supported the coup and had even helped the plotters, was trying to smuggle defeated opponents out of the city. At the time I heard this I had only marveled that such a system could so quickly become organized in a country where secrets are badly kept and where, for the last fifteen years, all political activities had taken place in the open. Never did I suspect that I would be needing those very services so soon.

Partly for the sake of trying a clandestine adventure, partly convinced by my father's arguments, I called the congressman, explained the situation and asked for a hundred-mile ride to Paracatu, the old mining town my father's family came from. I had some cousins there and felt that they could give me shelter and protection—though we had only met once.

The driver who was to take me across police roadblocks turned out to be an old acquaintance. He was one of those people you run into at bars where newsmen gather for small talk and long whiskies—a man with whom you drink, chat about politics, football, or films, but whom you can't say you really know.

We shook hands and, in the inevitable Volkswagen, proceeded to discover each other. The driver, a political stringer for country papers and a full-time civil servant—a frequent combination in Brazil—was part of a group of Socialist sympathizers who had set up the man-smuggling operation as soon as it became clear that Goulart was finished. To keep this underground railway going they were counting on the experience of some CP members, the generally pro-Goulart feelings of the minor bureaucrats who make up most of Brasília, and the anxiety of some conservative businessmen for their leftist relatives. One such businessman had even sent his firm's private plane to fetch his sister, a prominent local Communist. The plane landed on one of the many dirt roads that ring Brasília and took off again immediately, with the woman and two other persons on the military's

Most Wanted list. In record time the group set up a network of apartments and country houses, got hold of cars and whatever else was needed for whisking people out of the city.

This first plunge underground initiated me into a new world of political solidarity where people stood ready to take the gravest risks for ideas they believed in and for those who represented them. While I could easily understand the businessman's rescue of his sister—an act that fitted into my cultural background—the anonymous warriors for an abstract cause were a new experience for me, mysterious but highly appealing.

The driver left me, after a dusty zigzag around police outposts at the door of Major Jefferson Martins Ferreira's house in Paracatu. My cousin held this military title from the tradition of Brazil's backlands rather than from an academy. Since the days of the empire's civil wars, early in the nineteenth century, most rich landowners and merchants have been called "colonel" or "major," just as in the cities all well-dressed males over thirty are addressed as "doctor."

I was received naturally as if my grandfather had only yesterday moved to the coast and my family still lived next door. Shown into the dining room—where distinguished guests are received, the normal entrance to the household being the kitchen—I noticed, hanging over the table, a vast photograph of Carlos Lacerda, the coup's civilian leader and the most combative right-wing politician in the country. After relaxed but tireless inquiries about the health and doings of numerous other cousins who had also fled to the big cities on the seashore and noticing my inability to present objective information, Major Jefferson fell silent. The ceremonial rules of an agrarian society preclude any pressing of the guest to state his business for fear of making him feel unwelcome. Coming from a more hurried world, I explained why I was there—with a succinctness that went against all form. My eyes, as I spoke, wandered now and again to Lacerda's picture and I imagined my cousin's relief at the military takeover which would cut short all talk of agrarian reform and end any threats against his landholdings. But Major Jefferson didn't bat an eye as he heard me tell about my trip from Brasília, my attack on Vargas' minister, the wave of

arrests, my father's fears about the unleashed police. I might
have been talking about something that had happened on another planet. At no point, in the little he did say, was there a
hint that he might not help me for political reasons. I'm sure
such an idea never even crossed his mind. Having asked me if
I had enough money to hire a plane, he dispatched a boy
to call the pilot.

The "pilot" turned out to be an eighteen-year-old still
a few tests away from his license. The thought of him at the
controls disturbed me almost as much as the prospect of
flying three hundred miles through uncertain weather on a
canvas-winged Piper with no radio. However, as I was told
that he flew often and was still in one piece, I gathered my
courage and made arrangements to leave the next morning.

In the interior of Brazil a household is still a purely
masculine haven. Jefferson's sons came in for lunch—four
sturdy men, their revolvers hanging from their belts. They
inspected their city cousin with curious but belittling eyes.
Their experience was that this sort of visit always cost the
family something, either financially or politically. No relative would make the long trip back to the highlands for nothing. They knew that an arrival, especially if unannounced,
spelled the need for an extra effort on the part of the clan.

In Paracatu a newcomer is regarded with a mixture of
suspicion, curiosity and pride. Though Belo Horizonte, the
state capital, and even Rio de Janeiro are now within a
few hours' drive, the power centers, the pleasures and the
mysteries of a metropolis are still as remote to it as they had
been fifty years ago, when a trip on horseback took several
weeks and was generally one way, for the migrators would
seldom come back.

One of the duties of a visitor is to bring news of the
outside world. My cousins were happy to hear yarns of politics, social relations, and city customs from someone who
really lived it all, lending a touch of reality to what they
might have found in the outdated papers they so carefully
read. But even more than a provider of information, the city
relative is a prized source of prestige. His very existence
shows that the family is far-flung and that its name rings in
distant and glamorous circles. The reputation of home-town

sons is built up larger than life among local notables, who also share the glory, spiced by a dash of pique, of those who made good in Rio de Janeiro. Long after the guest's departure his visit will be discussed at night, or on the sidewalk wicker chairs, or before the drugstore or in the public square.

We sat around the table and talked. An antlike column of women kept coming from the kitchen with food, returning to the kitchen with dishes. I gorged on melting pork ribs, crisp fried chicken, fragrant black beans that smelled like childhood memories. I spun my tales between mouthfuls, skipping from stories about the most illustrious member of the clan, a senator-cousin who, as Foreign Minister, was a lasting glory even in retirement, to the details of recent events in Brasília. All the while I took the women for maids, though ill-trained ones, for they often giggled and were always eavesdropping and peeping from behind the doors. I vainly ascribed this behavior to the interest stirred by my presence. Something should have told me that a family made up only of men was peculiar, but I didn't bother to inquire where the womenfolk might be. Unconsciously I was slipping back into the mental ways of the old patriarchal society. Only next morning, when bidding my host farewell, did I discover that the shy woman I took for the cook was in fact his wife—and that the "maids" were my cousins, his daughters and in-laws. Even now they dared not address me, but pressed my hand good-by with downcast eyes.

CHAPTER III

ROOTS IN THE GROUND

Paracatu grew alongside a small river where gold had been found early in the eighteenth century. It was built on easy money and cheap labor. The first huts were quickly replaced by the two-story stone houses of rich merchants, mine owners, adventurous foreigners, and go-getting harlots who soon gathered there. The streets were paved with great granite slabs, laid by black slaves imported on foot from Bahia, a thousand miles away. The religious brotherhoods—in colonial Brazil, the centers of social life—competed with one another to build the most lavish churches. The town adopted for its patron St. Anthony of the Mango, a saint found nowhere else. A hospital, a school and the omnipresent tax-collection house of the Portuguese Crown were put up.

Prosperity lasted fifty years. Then, as gold grew scarce not only in the streams and open pits but also inside the mountains that the miners disemboweled, the town started downhill. The only families to stay were those that had gone into cattle ranching and agriculture. They and their servants kept up a pretense of life in a city where the liveliest realities were the ghosts of the past. Only in 1960, with the opening of the road from Rio to Brasília, did life stir again. Strangers were back, riding mammoth trucks, stopping for food and sleep, but moving on to a more modern Eldorado.

It was to a Paracatu whose fortunes were by then much declined that João de Melo Franco arrived by the turn of the eighteenth century. A Portuguese Roman Catholic priest, his interests were first gold, second women, and only third the salvation of his flock. It was not long before he had acquired a small fortune, a family, and the command of the local militia. He wore a sword over his cassock and organized dances and banquets in the orchard behind the house where his brood was multiplying.

Major Jefferson and I were offspring of this bellicose servant of the Church. Our family, as most old Brazilian families, cannot be scratched a few generations deep without unorthodox characters turning up—murderers, slave-traders, galley rowers, and women not always burdened by the weight of their honor. The people who came to America in the eighteenth century—willingly or by force—were the rebels of their times. Strong and aggressive, they infused the pre-existing settlements with their high spirits and lust for adventure. But they lived by a code of their own, one that would hardly be endorsed by the high-nosed descendants who trace back to it their claims to aristocracy. Snobbery is foolish anywhere—even in Britain, where it beefs up the tourist trade —but in young countries like Brazil it is ludicrous. Maybe this is why it is so widespread.

Discovering old bones in forgotten cupboards may be snobbishness under another guise, but it is one I find irresistible, for it is an unparalleled way to recognize the true face of a country's past. In the case of Brazil such old-bone hunts also teach one about the structure of colonial institutions.

I remember the pleasure with which I heard my mother tell about a grandparent of hers, one Januario Garcia, better known as Seven-Ears. This man used to till some land near the mining town of São João del Rey, in partnership with his younger brother. The two got into a dispute over farmstead markings with some neighbors and one day, returning from the market, the younger brother fell into an ambush: he was snatched from his horse, skinned, salted, and left bleeding on the road. Januario took after the murderers. He became a gang leader and rampaged all over the mining districts of Minas Geraes. Catching up with each of his brother's killers in turn, he would chop off the corpse's right ear and wear it on a string, gradually building up a mummified necklace. It took Januario several years to hunt down all seven murderers, and the family chronicle delicately leaves unexplained how all this time he provided for himself and his band. Public records are less restrained, however, and list against him several arrest orders for highway robbery, pillage, and such. His last recorded exploit was to surround Diamantina, a fairly big town that was the capital of the diamond-mine district, and hold it for ransom. Legend has it that his price was the life of the seventh and last of his younger brother's aggressors. The fact remains that Januario did catch and kill all seven—then retired to a placid family life. He died of old age.

The story of Januario Garcia offers just one illustration of how unfounded is the theory that describes the Brazilian character as nonviolent. The truth behind this assertion is simply this: Brazil has never known the violence of the oppressed. This is why outsiders and oppressors can see the masses as nonviolent, and, by praising their endurance, hope to keep them so.

No country in itself has a violent or nonviolent character. Only through circumstances do Germans and Spaniards differ from the Swiss. The now placid townsfolk of Fribourg and Zurich were for centuries the providers of Europe's most ruthless mercenaries and, during the nineteenth-century cantonal wars, joyfully broke one another's heads. The soulful, guitar-strumming Portuguese are today butchering enough freedom-fighters in Mozambique, Angola, and Guinea to bury once and for all their reputation for peacefulness. In Brazil the tradition of horizontal violence in struggles for local administrative power is reinforced by the habit of settling private odds directly, through gunfights and murders. As for vertical violence, that directed from above against the masses, it has never been anything but permanent. Taking the law into one's own hands results from the diffused presence of the state in the remote interior lands. There the police force, when it exists at all, tends to be corrupt and partisan. It enters into the clan structure of society and, rather than serving the community, it serves the dominant landowner. One cannot expect it to act with justice when his interests are at stake. On the other hand, it is used to keep the masses down, and the slightest sign of revolt is quashed at once. This goes for the peasant who asks for a larger share of his crop or some other betterment of his working conditions, as well as for the collective movements that, started by political or religious leaders, sometimes galvanize the masses and spread through the backlands.

Violence is a tool the ruling classes of Brazil have never ceased to use in defense of their privileges and property. Even the partisans of the nonviolent theory regarding the Brazilian people (and for "people" read "upper class") are undisturbed by police brutality against common criminals. Everyone has always known that thieves and, to a lesser degree, murderers (blood crimes being respected by the police) are tortured in station houses. Once the Rio police produced thirteen signed confessions for a supermarket holdup before hitting on the true robbers, who confessed without torture. Despite such occurrences the press never denounced such institutionalized outrages against the human person. Only when the Death Squadron[1] went a bit too far, committing with unnecessary barbarity an alarming number of executions and thereby shocking opinion abroad, did the Brazilian press voice some mild protest. The unavowed general attitude is that such dirty work is necessary to protect the "haves." Better let it be done discreetly and forget about it.

The same attitude applies to violence against workers and, especially, peasants. An example, among a great many: on December 24, 1967, Christmas festivities were taking place in the village of Vicencia, in the state of Pernambuco. Among the celebrants was a peasant who, having been ordered off a plot he had worked for ten years, obstinately refused to leave—even after the landowners had unroofed his house. The landowners, flanked by bodyguards, kidnaped the man in full view of the townsfolk and his family. His body

[1] The Death Squadrons are police gangs that do away with common law and political prisoners on the pretext that law courts let them off too lightly. In point of fact they sell protection to drug peddlers and wipe out criminal gangs they have no business relations with. They operate mainly in Rio and São Paulo and are credited with more than one thousand executions since 1965. The names of Death Squadron leaders are known—such as Sergio Fleury, São Paulo's star killer—but nothing is done about them because they make themselves useful by carrying out political murders for the regime. The Paris newspaper Le Monde of April 27, 1971, ran a good account of the Death Squadron's organization and history.

was found days later, without eyes, nose or lips. The murderers were not arrested. Questioned by the police, one of them stated that the idea had merely been to give the peasant a scare by holding a dagger to his neck—but that, alas, the jeep they were riding in bumped on a rock, the dagger jumped, a carotid was severed. Not a single newspaper printed a word about this at the time. Months later, the police report having been filed, a squib came out in small print.

The patronage system of Brazil's backwoods politics is a permanent source of disputes and vendettas. Even in state capitals bullets often prevail over ballots. In Maceió, capital of Alagoas, the state assembly was invaded on September 13, 1957, by a band of machine-gun-toting deputies. The governor's impeachment was to be voted on during that session, there being strong circumstantial evidence that he had ordered the murder of an opposition assemblyman. The crime had been so much expected that the victim, a doctor, sent to the Minister of Justice and other federal authorities a prophetic description of his own death. He said he would be ambushed some night at his front door, returning from a medical visit. The murder took place in just that way and it shook the country's political circles. The governor lost his majority at the assembly and his supporters decided against risking a vote on his impeachment. They chose instead, before any debate could get started, to open fire on their colleagues. Thirteen were left wounded and one dead. After a brief federal intervention, the governor got a court order reinstating him and he happily finished his term. In later years, however, his family was all but wiped out by killers, who did not spare even old women and children.

In Minas Geraes, a state regarded as "civilized," trigger politics of this sort is not uncommon. My grandfather, who for thirty years represented in Congress the district of Montes Claros, a ranching area, used to tell blood-curdling tales about life in the backlands. Both his parents plus a daughter and two servants had been axed to death. The surviving kinsmen ascribed the murders to the rival Prates family and launched a feud that was to last forty years and, in the end, forced both clans out of town.

Heading our clan's forces was my grandfather's sister-in-law, Dona Tiburtina. I saw her only once, a few months before her death. She was a frail old lady, wrapped in a shawl-like ankle-length black dress. Her whitish hair was tied in a bun at the back of her head and all she had was a lonely tooth in the middle of her mouth. Her voice was a whisper. She spoke in baby talk: "My little son, you must eat a tiny bit more of this nice little food." I found it hard to conceive that this diminutive woman, obviously incapable of hurting a fly, had lived up to her reputation.

Dona Tiburtina's greatest exploit happened in 1930, during the campaign that preceded rigged presidential elections and the take-over by Getúlio Vargas. The Prates had cast their lot with the federal government while the Alves had sided with Vargas and the opposition. Montes Claros' local dispute became a central issue in the state. The city, whose prosperity was evidenced by its countless brothels and gambling houses, was the key to the entire northern territory, an area of some hundred thousand square miles that spread to the neighboring state of Bahia. Accordingly it merited the visit of the Vice-President. He arrived with what in those days amounted to the full regalia of power: a special train and a military band. Welcomed by his Prates supporters he proceeded to the main square followed by a firecracking procession. Tiburtina's house was packed with armed relatives and bodyguards. As the procession wended past the house the firecrackers popped with renewed fervor, humiliating the enemy in their suggestion of impending triumph. One went off at the feet of Tiburtina's husband, who was watching from the doorway. Seeing him limp into the garden she assumed he was wounded. She gave the order to fire. The volley that ensued, leaving two dead and several wounded, echoed over Brazil as the first announcement of the coming revolution. The Vice-President was hurt in the neck by bone fragments, and scrambled to safety—indeed with such haste that his train *backed* out of the city, a face-losing procedure that shifted many of the town's allegiances.

The strong-arm activities of Tiburtina and her relatives did not sit well with my grandfather, a mild and absent-minded country doctor whose obsession was chess. As a congressman he lived in Rio, far from the seething hatreds of

Montes Claros, which he only visited between sessions. He confined his parliamentary activities to the budget and transport committees, in both of which he strove to obtain the maximum federal help for his constituency. He hardly cared about the great political issues of the day, and the records show little trace of his interventions. My grandfather was the type of representative I was to find still formed the majority of the House two political generations later—men from underdeveloped areas, closely dependent on local power centers and concerned primarily with drawing federal money for their districts, where the infrastructure of progress (roads, schools, hospitals, even factories) can be built only with federal aid.

A country doctor whose practice was for many years the only one in the region, could aspire to a certain freedom from the big landowners who controlled most of the voters. My grandfather loved his practice and kept it alive during his annual visits, though I wonder how people survived during his eight months' absence. He enjoyed telling about his medical experiences, dwelling in loving detail on how to remove a man's leg with a carpenter's saw and on other such sidelights of the trade. A favorite story of his was how he had once been summoned by some muleteers gathered round a sick man, under a big mango tree on a godforsaken track in the highlands. Dismounting, he at once saw that the man suffered from a purulent glaucoma that should be operated on immediately. He made the patient down as much rum as he could hold, cleaned the blade of his penknife on a flame, then neatly pulled the eye out. He would liven the description by poking a finger against his socket and saying, "See, it came out just like that, a whole round eye, this big!" I would look and imagine the gluelike round gelatin ball in the hollow of his fingers—and run away screaming. This eighteenth-century tale happened a mere fifty years ago, and may well be taking place again today, somewhere in Brazil's wastes.

Most underdeveloped countries show a striking contrast between the large cities and the agrarian back country. In Brazil this contrast is so sharp that some sociologists have adopted the thesis of a dual society with a modern, industrialized, capitalistic pole developing in a way similar to the United States and Europe, in opposition to a stagnant, feudalistic, agrarian countryside. This analysis, in my view, suffers from bad focusing. Brazil is integrated lock, stock, and barrel in the capitalistic world—and both its "pole of development" and its "pole of backwardness" are inescapable consequences of this integration.[2] But the fact is that life in the cities—where are concentrated the dominant elites, foreign heads of businesses, professional men of every kind, and in general the cultural, commercial, and industrial establishments—is many worlds and generations apart from life in the bulk of the country.

This gulf between rich and poor areas also helps shape the political attitude of the elite. In São Paulo, Rio de Janeiro, and other more developed regions, holders of economic power are seldom drawn to politics. They represent the more dynamic economic sectors and are part of a modern and international world. Their wealth is a key to any door. They defend their interests behind the scenes, lobbying in their clubs, their yachts, their country houses. They shy clear of the risks and publicity of a political career, preferring to finance the ambitions of docile professionals, generally lawyers. Public office hinders rather than aids the maintenance

[2] For the dual society theory see Jacques Lambert, *Os Dois Brasis*, São Paulo, Revista dos Tribunais, 1959; Charles Wagley, *An Introduction to Brazil*, New York, Columbia University Press, 1963, and virtually all published analyses that study the country from an anthropological point of view. For the counter-arguments about feudalism and the history of Brazil's integration in the Western World's economic structure, see Celso Furtado, *The Economic Growth of Brazil, a Survey from Colonial to Modern Times*, Berkeley, University of California Press, 1963; Caio Prado, Jr., *Formação do Brasil Contemporaneo*, São Paulo, ed. Brasiliense, 9th ed., 1965; and, dealing at length with this question, André Gunther Frank, *Capitalism and Underdevelopment in Latin America*, New York, Monthly Review Press, 1967, chapters III and IV. Required reading for anyone interested in Latin American economic history is Stanley and Barbara Stein, *The Colonial Heritage of Latin America*, New York, Oxford University Press, 1970, which contains some highly penetrating analyses on the Continent's development; Nicos Poulantzas's *Pouvoir Politique et Classes Sociales de l'État Capitaliste*, Paris, Maspero, 1968, discusses from a theoretical viewpoint the causes for coexisting forms of production in a given economic system.

or increase of their power. In the country's underdeveloped interior the situation is reversed. A political career leads to wealth and provides one with the means to keep it. Scarcer opportunities tend to cluster in fewer hands. A seat in Congress or in a state assembly is an important asset that the local plutocracy cannot afford to vest in strangers. When a big landowner refrains from running for Congress it is not because he thinks, as does his urban counterpart, that checkbooks work better than speeches. He does so through fear that he, a stammering redneck, hasn't the rhetoric to compete with the well-educated professionals. Since the parliamentarian tool must not be wasted he tries to marry off a daughter or a beloved niece to someone able to represent him, and then goes about having the in-law elected. Only when this fails does he reach outside the family circle, the man chosen being normally a lawyer, doctor, or army officer. In the past he could also be a priest, but ecclesiastics are today deemed unreliable, some ordained members of the Catholic Church having lately acquired the scurvy habit of siding with the oppressed.

The opposed postures of the Brazilian elite toward politics are reflected in the social evolution of the great Paraíba Valley coffee barons.[3] None of them became senators, representatives, or ministers. Only after the land grew barren did their descendants, already stripped of the sonorous titles the emperor had wisely bestowed upon a single generation, try their luck in the "system" and join the ranks of the juridical parasites. In my mother's family, for instance, the coffee wealth amassed by slave labor was sufficient to protect four generations of prolific males from politics and work.

The patriarch of my family, who so well shielded his lin-

[3] The Paraíba Valley runs through the early coffee lands of the state of Rio de Janeiro and São Paulo. During the second half of the nineteenth century it became the richest part of Brazil and accounted for much of the empire's export earnings. Its landed aristocracy accumulated huge wealth and played an economic role similar to that of the owners of the sugar-cane plantations in the Northeast during the sixteenth and seventeenth centuries. An excellent portrait of the social and economic structures of the valley appears in Stanley Stein, *Vassouras, a Brazilian Coffee Country: 1850–1900*, Cambridge, Harvard University Press, 1957.

eage from the hazards of breadwinning was typical of the valley's pioneer strain. By the age of twenty-five he had already made a fortune carting goods from the coast and trading with the decaying gold towns of Minas Geraes. While in Rio, between mule convoys, he joined in the drunken escapades led by Pedro I, Brazil's first emperor. Brawling and whoring were a good entree to the court. Through his friendship with the prince he became the crown's chief moneylender. Such were the interests he collected that when Pedro was forced to abdicate and left for new adventures and revolutions in Portugal, the social-climbing muleskinner had enough capital to start a coffee plantation. He broke land on the Rio Preto and, twenty years later, was producing fifteen hundred tons of coffee, owned several hundred slaves, a baron's crown and a palace with no verandas, put up by a French architect with haughty disregard for the sizzling tropical sun. He had meanwhile also acquired a submissive wife, 2 legitimate children and 101 recorded illegitimate ones, mostly mulatto. He died from a heart attack at the age of fifty-five, while he was attempting to drive a visitor around his plantation in a carriage drawn by untamed colts.

When I crawled into the canvas plane that was to take me from Paracatu to an active political life in April 1964, I carried with me, like a kind of protective coat of privileges, this background of soldier-priests, cutthroats, country doctors, and rakish barons. Normally these privileges would have meant a life in the service of the establishment, sharing its profits and pleasures. The raw truths of Brazil were to turn me, as they did so many other privileged Brazilians, into a traitor to my class. We chose to fight with our people, to transform our society, to liberate our country. In the process we were to meet with prison, exile, torture, and death. But we were also to find joy, companionship, a purpose in life and, in my own case, faith. These are sufficient rewards for any human being.

CHAPTER IV

MILITARY POWER

It is amazing how well small planes can fly over the vast wastes of underdeveloped countries. In the interior of Brazil where, during the rainy season, roads are long, muddy traps, planes are the only reliable means of transportation. People who have never seen a car walk into them with nonchalance. The Xavantes Indians of the Amazon basin think planes are indestructible. Plane crashes are not part of their experience. They say: "A bird falls when you strike it with an arrow, but planes never fall, no matter how many arrows you throw at them." And they are right. Though maintenance standards are rather low, there are surprisingly few accidents. On the flat swamplands of Mato Grosso, farmers inspect their cattle and crops from the air, housewives shop by plane, and children learn to fly at an age when suburban teen-agers don't yet have a chance at the wheel of the family car. The old DC-3's the Air Force flies to the western forest outposts are the only link between forgotten populations and the urban centers. Even bishops have to use Cessnas and Beechcrafts during their annual visits to missionary parishes. In fact, some American missionaries have been accused of smuggling gold, gems, and atomic minerals out of the country in their church-owned planes. Most smuggling is airborne, and in some northern and western regions it is the most prosperous commercial activity. In the territory of Rio Branco alone, bordering the Guianas, there are more than two hundred illegal airstrips, some big enough to receive a four-engined plane.

My teen-aged pilot negotiated three hours of bumpy

flight to Belo Horizonte with great ease. He dropped me at the air club and left in a hurry: he was nervous about being asked for his license. The police, because of the political troubles, kept an eye on the normally abandoned field. There was no other transportation at hand, so I ended my first underground trip by hitchhiking to town in a patrol car.

Seen from the air most Brazilian cities look like the concentric rings of a solar eclipse. There is a dark central core of apartment buildings, two-story houses, and well-paved streets and avenues. Here are the residences of the upper and middle classes and the location of commercial activities. The lighter outer circle is formed by the makeshift dwellings of the poor, the *favelas*, where the human waves that have fled the interior stop. Here survival is a ceaseless battle for the left-over scraps of the center.

Rapid urban growth has planted these miserable rings everywhere. When the marginal populations conquer a foothold too close to the privileged, by putting up their shacks on slopes once too steep for economic building, the government removes them forcibly to low-income housing projects. Within these projects, often financed by American funds, transportation is scarce and jobs even more so. Sometimes the round-trip bus fare to work will cost a quarter of a family's monthly income. People are forced to move not only for the benefit of possible real-estate developers or the aesthetic pleasure of sentimental tourists, but also for the tranquillity of military staffs, who view shantytowns as security risks and possible bases for urban guerrillas.[1] Their fear may be well founded. Shantytowns and marginal populations—people squeezed out of the country's economic life—are necessary consequences of the savage capitalism their guns protect.

In the countryside peasants are condemned by a land tenure system of large holdings to a slow starving death. In the cities they fare little better, for the country's industrial

[1] Jerome Levinson and Juan de Onís' book *The Alliance That Lost Its Way* (Chicago, Quadrangle Books, 1970, pp. 255–278) describes how ineffectually reformist and reactionary governments in Latin America have tried to cope, aided by North American money, with the continent's urban explosion.

structure cannot offer them enough jobs. While the share of industrial output in Brazil's gross national product is, at 30 per cent, roughly that of France, less than 9 per cent of the labor force is employed by industry, as compared to over 25 per cent in most developed countries. The reason is that even with the prevailing starvation wages, government subsidies make it cheaper to import labor-saving machines than to employ people. On the other hand, the existence of vast unemployed masses—what Marx called an industrial reserve army—hinders wage increases and is a threat against a too militant labor movement. For every unskilled job offered there are dozens of candidates. Employers hope that those lucky enough to get one will think twice before risking it by striking for a raise or better work conditions. These conditions give Brazil, the most industrialized country on the Continent, the dubious distinction of having the lowest average industrial wages in all Latin America.[2]

Belo Horizonte, although it is Brazil's first planned city, nonetheless follows the urban mushroom pattern. Built to be a modest administrative capital, in seventy years it swelled to a million and a half inhabitants, developed an industrial belt and a commercial district spiked with futuristic skyscrapers. But its people have kept small-town habits, such as the Sunday evening strolls through the gardens before the governor's palace, which is the traditional meeting place for young lovers.

Social life is segregated. Members of the financial and bureaucratic elite generally know and visit one another. They belong to the same country clubs and keep the same habits. They consider marriages, baptisms, and burials as great occasions to meet, show off new dresses and exchange gossip. Men discuss politics at bars and cafes, where a female presence, though now tolerated, is still a sensation. Football matches at the immense stadium provide the possibility for contact among different social classes in the same way as do the beaches in Rio and other coastal cities.

Families have close relationships and still call nightly on

[2] According to the New York *Times* (January 25, 1971) the average hourly wage of a Brazilian industrial worker is, at 31 cents, half that of a Mexican and one cent less than that of a Paraguayan.

friends and relatives for long chats over coffee cups. Maidens still flirt at the garden gate, under the watchful eyes of mothers and aunts who believe their surveillance a better insurance against scandals than a daily pill.

The sexual inhibitions of Latin American societies are a consequence of our traditionally schizophrenic upbringing. Machismo calls us to raise our sons to lay every woman they cross, while family honor rests on a girl's hymen. We teach our daughters to guard their virginity as fiercely as a Roman vestal. Then we wonder about neurosis. . . . I once teased the wife of a friend for her strict vigilance over her daughters' suitors. Though she was quite open-minded on other matters, she allowed the girls to see their boy friends only according to a strict ritual and a precisely kept schedule. They had two hours for love-talking on Fridays and a little more on Saturdays and Sundays. Their geographic wanderings were also prescribed: at first they met at the gate; as the courtship blossomed they could use the veranda; and admittance to the living room, the home's sanctum sanctorum, came only after the engagement was formally announced. The arguments I used to attack this obsolete setup left my friend unmoved. She stared coldly and said, "Everyone knows very well how to raise other people's daughters."

The shantytown masses have little effect on Belo Horizonte's inner circles. They hang onto the outskirts of the city, working at the steel and textile mills, providing domestic help and such services as shoeshining and car washing. Their presence is felt by the stress they put on public services and as human streams on the sidewalks. For the closely knit dominant groups, they are merely faceless bodies. The few that break through the barriers, by luck or hard work, quickly forget their origins.

I had some friends in this self-protective society and could also count on a valuable asset—the governor's protection. This was important at the time, for he had been the civil architect of the military conspiracy, turning Minas Geraes into the physical base from which the first troops marched against Goulart.

I had first seen Governor Magalhães Pinto many years before, when as an upcoming congressman and already prosperous small banker he was starting a political career under the guidance of Virgilio de Melo Franco.[3]

My contacts with Magalhães Pinto developed from these early contacts to a more sustained relationship in Congress, where I reported for some time. When Jânio Quadros ran for President in 1960, I followed his campaign but was later switched to cover the state election in Minas Geraes which promised a closer race and also had national importance.

A political campaign in the interior has little to do with politicking in the developed world. It is an exhausting marathon over a territory the size of France. Scattered towns and villages are linked by roads no better than dirt tracks. Hotels are rare and when they exist are hardly up to hygienic standards. You do not rent a room but a bed, which you sometimes share with chickens or, if unlucky, with a strayed pig. The whole time-consuming process is inefficient but the candidate has to go through it in homage to the local notables, who still hold electoral power in the backlands and insist on having personal contacts with him.

The candidate can only take a few people with him— no more than two if he happens to fly a small plane. Representatives of the national press are high up on his priority list, for he depends on them to spread his statements to audiences larger than the thin crowds he faces. He goes to great lengths to accommodate reporters and their relations become close, often intimate. For days and weeks they

[3] Virgilio, a cousin of my father's, was a conservative politician with some social preoccupations and a broad following among anti-Vargas students. A liberal in the twenties, he had been one of the youthful leaders of the 1930 revolution, but soon broke with Vargas, who would not appoint him governor of Minas Geraes. He had become an efficient organizer for the Liberal democratic reaction that finally ended Vargas' dictatorship. He had been a co-founder of the UDN, National Democratic Union, the most powerful conservative party in Brazil which was later to provide most of the civilian conspirators for the 1964 coup. An exceedingly charming man, hunter, gentleman farmer, ladies' man, an indefatigable conversationalist, he influenced a generation of young professionals who sourly turned to the extreme right as they gathered age, wealth, and electoral defeats. Governor Magalhães Pinto was one of these men. He was a member of the UDN and a millionaire.

travel, eat, and sometimes lodge together, getting to know each other's tastes and eccentricities.

It was this kind of relationship I had struck with Governor Magalhães Pinto during his bid for public favor. I was now ready to cash in on it. I knew he was a cautious and selfish politician who would not run great risks to help me but would remove the threats if they were mild.

The threats I sensed were, in fact, nonexistent. As so many conceited people were doing during the first days of the military take-over, I was overvaluing my own importance on the police's priority list. The governor received me promptly, wrote the laissez-passer I had asked for on a visiting card, and rounded out by inviting me to dinner. In less than seventy-two hours I had gone underground, found shelter under the old family tree, flown clandestinely into a state capital, all to be red-carpeted back into the establishment. No amateurish Scarlet Pimpernel could have done better. By nightfall I had sent an article to my paper and was sitting at a formal dining table, next to General Carlos Luiz Guedes, the military satrap of Belo Horizonte, having my first direct exposure to barracks philosophy.

Brazilian generals are a garrulous breed. All their lives they have to listen in silence to their superiors. Yet it seems that the acquisition of the stars of command demolishes some inner dam in their brains, letting loose an unending torrent of words. At last they can speak. At last their rank assures them a captive audience. Life-long habits of listening are filed away forever.

I marveled, during dinner, at the general's loquacity and tried to follow his jargon. He explained at length why the pro-Goulart cavalry regiments in the South had to surrender without fighting. He drew maps with his fork on the tablecloth. Fruits and glasses were the troops. It made me think of some old film mocking retired Indian Service officers describing their battles to bored colleagues in a Pall Mall club. Guedes kept referring to armored and hippo regiments. It took me some time to understand that the Brazilian army had two types of cavalry troops, mechanized and horseback. Apparently only those on horseback—the hippo regiments—

sided with Goulart and they had no intention of re-enacting the Polish charge against Hitler's Panzer divisions.

General Guedes had a reputation for intelligence and honesty. It struck me that when civilians speak of an "intelligent general" they use the adjective more generously than when speaking of civilians. What is really meant is that so-and-so is intelligent *for a general*. Considering that the Brazilian military were largely responsible for establishing some of the country's best technological institutions and most of its basic industries, this prejudice may seem unfair. Unfortunately, one has only to talk to our generals or read their patriotic proclamations to understand why the fact of their intelligence should be accepted only with serious reservations.

Any special claim to honesty among Brazil's military elite can scarcely be better established than one to intelligence. Compared to the military of some other Latin American countries, the Brazilian brass are truly virtuous. They have never engaged in mass corruption or endowed themselves with immense privileges, as, for instance, their Venezuelan counterparts. Brazil has never had a Batista, a Trujillo, a Perez Jimenez or a Peron. However, corruption does flourish. There is today seldom a financial scandal in which some high brass are not involved. The wheeling and dealing at the Ministry of Public Works is the most spectacular, as is illustrated by the multimillion-dollar swindle of the Rio-Niteroi bridge project.[4] More modest kickbacks for favors on public contracts are not exceptional. In at least one case the fast money ended up financing subversive groups. A frontman charged by the secret services with depositing the money in a Swiss bank, a clerk known among revolutionaries as the "Good Bourgeois," decided on a more patriotic destination for his masters' savings and ended up at the Navy's intelligence center. Subjected to electric shocks while

[4] The Rio-Niteroi bridge is a ninety-million-dollar prestige project. It stopped when workers and engineers died during a security test that proved the foundations to be unsafe. The constructing firm was deemed unworthy to do business with the government but its managers were not criminally prosecuted. The minister responsible for the fiasco kept his post.

hanging upside down, he told all he knew. The regime's *petite histoire* holds his confession (involving the President's family in the plot) as one cause for President Costa e Silva's sudden brain stroke. The facts are that the story was hushed, the government refused to release him in January 1971 as part of the kidnaped Swiss ambassador's ransom and no satisfactory explanation was given for the source of the two million dollars the Good Bourgeois was said to have handed guerrilla groups.

More sophisticated forms of corruption like influence peddling have also become standard practice. Large corporations, foreign and national, compete in hiring generals and colonels as public relations officers to strengthen their leverage when bidding for public contracts.

Most of Castelo Branco's ministers fit comfortably into this scheme. General Golbery Couto e Silva, for instance, left his post as head of the National Information Service, the local CIA, to become president of Dow Chemicals in Brazil. Others have found shelter with Mercedes-Benz, Ericson, and even Spanish firms. Colonel Costa e Silva, the ex-President's son, became an instant millionaire during his father's rule. His mother can now even afford to outbid museums for a Blue Period Picasso.

Expense accounts, long-legged secretaries, chauffered limousines, and the magic status symbol of successful businessmen—the company-paid Diner's Club credit card—have proved irresistible temptations to some officers having their first taste of high living. After all, the military took power in order to ensure the survival of the capitalist system in Brazil, so it's hardly surprising that they feel compelled to share in the benefits.

Brazil's military men are no more—and possibly no less —honest than the average urban-lower middle-class citizen, which is the social origin of most of them.[5] They have the

---

[5] The best study of Brazil's military establishment and the only one available in English is Alfred Stepans, *The Military in Politics, Changing Patterns in Brazil*, Princeton, Princeton University Press, 1971. He notes that army officers are recruited mostly from urban-lower middle-class families. There are only a few from working-class or peasant backgrounds. Upper-class origins are also rare.

same political vacillations and opportunist tendencies as other members of their class. They also follow Latin America's middle-class social-climbing tendencies by striving to acquire and by supporting upper-class values and objectives.

The majority of Brazil's officer corps have undefined political attitudes. The highly politicized pre-1964 elections for the Military Club were always a battle between a nationalistic, social-minded minority and a pro-American, reactionary minority.[6] Both groups courted the favors of the neutral majority, known as "Partido do Muro," the party of those who sat on the wall waiting to see on which side power would fall. That each group won out in alternation shows the opportunism of most officers. It also indicates that the two small groups of politically motivated activists were well balanced. So well, in fact, that a sociologist once proclaimed that "the stability of democratic institutions is ensured in inverse proportion to the unity of the Armed Forces," an axiom applicable not only to Brazil. As soon as the pro-American group could utilize a momentary unity in the Armed Forces to seize power, not only were democratic institutions wiped out, but the political balance within the military establishment was also destroyed by a series of purges aimed at guaranteeing the dictatorship's survival. The post-1964 purges were the first in Brazilian history to expel a sizable part of the officer corps for political reasons. Similar measures taken in the twenties against a group of lieutenants who organized several rebellions were limited to those who had actually taken up arms against the government. The accused then were given ample defense opportunities and their cases were heard before the country's courts of justice. After 1964 the purges affected greater numbers—almost 10 per cent of the Army's officers—and were based exclusively on secret records. No reasons were given for punishments. According to the military-issued Institutional Acts, the courts of justice were prevented from passing judgment on their legality.

In early April 1964, the ultimate victory of the pro-

[6] Elections for the Military Club, to which all officers belong, are the only way of periodically assessing the political wood of the military in Brazil.

American military group through the coup d'état was far from clear, even when Marshal Castelo Branco published his choice of ministers. They seemed to be a particularly old and conservative group, traditionally connected to the UDN. The bond that truly tied them together was lost to most observers. Only later, as administrative policies stabilized and an army of American counselors invaded every key office in the Ministries of Finance and Planning, did we find the way out of the labyrinth through a thread that led to the Escola Superior de Guerra (ESG), Brazil's War College.

The ESG, better known as the "Sorbonne," is a Cold War offspring. Founded in 1949 by General Cordeiro de Farias, an officer with a long political career and militantly pro-American position, its task is to form a knowledgeable anti-Communist elite, capable of running the country according to strategic goals defined by the General Staff. Its courses deal with economic and social problems as well as military ones, for every aspect of national life is considered open to attack by subversive forces led by International Communism. Pupils are career officers, from colonels up, and highly placed civilians, roughly in equal proportions. The civilians are bankers, diplomats, engineers, civil servants, and conservative parliamentarians, but not labor leaders or socialist-leaning politicians. In the words of General Juarez Tavora, one of the school's commanders, they might bring difficulties to the desired companionship among members of the staff. In fact, they are considered impossible to brainwash into the school's elitist models.

The ESG had graduated 1,814 pupils by 1969, an average of 90 per year, and its alumni association, ADESG, had become one of the country's foremost power centers. It often hands out public statements on national policies, serving as a channel of expression for high-ranking military, who would otherwise be prevented by disciplinary rules from interfering in political discussions. It has also secured privileges for its members. The most important is the legal possibility offered to civilian alumni to become security officers in ministries and important authorities, posts normally restricted to officers.

Since its foundation there has always been a member of

the American military mission to Brazil attached as liaison officer to the ESG's staff. He has unlimited access to documents and lectures. On one occasion this foreign presence was cause for a small scandal: Senator Aurelio Viana, a labor representative from Rio, noticed a uniformed American officer at a top secret briefing by the Foreign Minister. He protested, but the school's commander, General Castelo Branco, assured him that there were no secrets in Brazil from our American allies. Unconvinced, the senator publicly tore up his membership card and denounced the case to the press.

The U.S. government considers the ESG such an important political tool for furthering its interests in Brazil that John Kennedy found time, at the heart of the Cuban missile crisis, to welcome its members to the White House. In fact, these annual VIP trips to the United States are a fundamental part of the methods used by the American military to seduce their Latin colleagues. In the words of General George Beatty, chairman of the U. S. Delegation at the Joint Brazil-U. S. Military Commission, "Orientation visits provide a unique opportunity to acquaint selected groups of current and future leaders with U.S. culture, technology and government. To the staff and command schools, these visits mean knowledge of the United States at a formative time of the officers' development. To the high-level civilians and military of the War College, orientation visits furnish a broad insight of the United States at a time when the national and international interests of their country are under discussion and review. The magnitude, extent and costs of the U.S. defense effort are brought dramatically to their attention during visits to defense installations. Their recognition of this magnitude has been very influential in persuading the Brazilians that the U.S. strategic capabilities enable them to keep their military equipment procurement primarily limited to their needs for internal security and defense of contiguous maritime communications."[7]

Translating the foregoing into everyday language, Gen-

7 "U. S. Policies and Programs in Brazil," hearings before the Sub-Committee on Western Hemisphere Affairs, U. S. Senate, May 4, 5 and 11, 1971, p. 55.

eral Beatty said that by showing rockets, IBM computers, sophisticated radar systems, and nuclear warheads to the Brazilians, U.S. military men had convinced them to leave their international protection in American hands and concentrate on policing their own countrymen.

A "national security doctrine" slowly evolved from the Escola Superior de Guerra's activities. It is based on two postulates: 1) a Third World War between Western Christian civilization, led by the United States, on the one hand, and the forces of atheistic communism, led by the Soviet Union, on the other, is inevitable and, 2) in such a war, the forces of second-rate powers such as Brazil will be unable even to play the auxiliary role they had fulfilled during World War II. Their task will be to police their own territories against a novel form of warfare promoted by ideological antagonism: internal subversion. In short, the armies of satellite countries lost the traditional role of defenders of their frontiers and became huge police forces with the right to control all aspects of the country's life. Though the fallacy of this "World War III" theory became apparent even to a casually informed public after the U.S.-U.S.S.R. entente that ended the 1962 Cuban missile crisis, and the growing Sino-Soviet conflict, it was not abandoned by Brazilian generals and their North American friends. The reason is simple—if the unlikelihood of a war were to be acknowledged, the military would be gradually deprived of influence and their slice of the national budget. For career officers such an acknowledgment would mean that their training, their drab exercises, their whole lives, were meaningless. This was a reality they could not face and one, indeed, that any professional group could not but reject. Only two viable choices, both ideological, were open to them: the Armed Forces could become the leader of an independent Socialist nation, or the ruling policemen of the status quo.

A society shapes its armed defenders after the image of its ruling class. For most officers the policeman role was the surest way of assuming total power over the country as well as the choice best fitted to their political outlook.

The choice of an all-embracing national security function for the Armed Forces, one that became generalized after the coup, had long been the goal of ESG's staff. When, in the surprise of lightning victory, the military had to reach quick agreement on a future course to follow, only the ESG program had sufficient support and scope to be adopted.

Brazil's populist governments had since 1950 committed the fatal error of reserving troop commands for nationalist officers while relinquishing the military schools to the most reactionary ones. From this privileged position they indoctrinated several military generations. Thus a policy meant to guarantee the regime from conspirators proved in the long run to be its undoing.

The American military mission to Brazil not only backed the ESG but trained as many Brazilians as it could in the United States and the Panama Canal Zone. From 1950 to 1970 this training program reached 6,858 officers and enlisted men, a high number considering that there are only about 13,500 officers on active duty in the Brazilian Army. Also, the American military assistance program to Brazil is by far the largest in Latin America, totaling 221 million U.S. dollars during the same period. After 1960 most of this "aid" consisted of anti-guerrilla material, which is inexpensive compared to the prestige-building hardware—tanks, jet-bombers, carriers—preferred by underdeveloped military men in the past.

Brazil's dictatorship has relied on American backing ever since it came to power. For the first time in diplomatic history the State Department did not wait for the head of state to be officially replaced before recognizing the new political realities. Lyndon Johnson's congratulations reached the mutinous generals while João Goulart was still in Brazil. The embassy's staff was immediately beefed up with administrative experts who started to work in governmental offices on the same footing as the top Brazilian bureaucrats. The military mission soon became the third largest in the world, after Vietnam and India. Credits, frozen during Goulart's last months in office, were showered on the country's new financial managers. The once forbidding doors of the International Monetary Fund and the World Bank were suddenly thrown open. Rio became such a popular resort for North American high officials that the crews of a few battleships that had been secretly hanging off the coast for a possible intervention were almost lost in the crowd. Lincoln Gordon, the American ambassador, unbashfully praised the military government, going so far as to call the coup one of the century's turning points for the cause of democracy. His presence on the Brazilian political scene was so obtrusive that some irreverent students painted a slogan on the walls: "Enough of middlemen—Lincoln Gordon for president."

The early official American approval of the dictatorship still prevails today—if anything, reinforced—though the true barbarous nature of the regime is now so notorious that not even its stanchest friends can deny it.

In 1970 a "fact-finding" mission of the U. S. House of Representatives went to Brazil. Like most of these tourist enterprises it stayed only a few days, later collecting its newly acquired wisdom into a publication. It approvingly quotes the views it got from the local American military personnel: "Military personnel to whom we spoke see Brazilian officers as one of the best educated and informed social groups in the country and, more than any other group, dedicated to national rather than regional and personal interests. Their withdrawal from the political arena is not seen as occurring in the near future. For that reason they emphasize the continued importance of the military assistance training program as a means of exerting U.S. influence and retaining the current pro-U.S. attitude of the Brazilian Armed Forces."[8]

At the time I was having dinner with General Guedes at the state house of Minas Geraes, the extent of U.S. involvement with the new government was still unclear and the ESG's projects for long-term military rule were unknown to all except a tight inner group of alumni. We were all prisoners of a less sophisticated past. Brazilian dominant classes still believed in influencing and interpreting the country's life according to a traditional social pattern, in which a protracted military dictatorship was unthinkable. Very few realized that the liberal-democratic period of Brazilian his-

[8] "Report of the Special Study Mission to Latin America." Subcommittee on National Security Policy and Scientific Development, Committee on Foreign Affairs, House of Representatives, Washington, D.C., May 7, 1970, p. 5.

tory was over. It was buried with João Goulart's political bones. Almost no one imagined the hardships of times to come—the terrorist police state, the revolutionary struggles against it—that closed forever an epoch of compromise and enthroned naked force as the one tool for maintaining or challenging the political organizations of our country.

CHAPTER V

HIS MASTER'S VOICE

Freedom of the press generally means the publisher's freedom to print his political opinions and forward his financial interests. Opinions in the Brazilian press are in general reactionary and interests seldom avowable. The archetype of the press baron was Assis Chateaubriand, a brilliant privateer who built from scratch the country's largest communications empire, acquiring in the process a senator's seat, a magnificent collection of paintings, and an ambassadorship to the Court of St. James's. He had odd reasons for defending capitalism and foreign investments. I once heard him saying to ex-Finance Minister Santiago Dantas, also a self-made man, but one who had social preoccupations: "If it were not for the rich and the foreign businessmen, where would smart penniless men like you and me get our money from?"

Chateaubriand assumed that his employees would follow his example and use their jobs to wring sinecures and favors from politicians, so he deliberately kept their wages low, setting an example only too gladly followed by the rest of the industry. In Brazil journalist guilds seemed always able to obtain petty privileges for their members, such as income-tax deductions and cut-rate fares on international flights, but could never force newspaper owners to pay decent salaries. Also publishers never allow their journalists to defend dissident ideas. No wonder then that journalism rates low in prestige as compared to other liberal professions. Only recently has the appearance of huge, modern-minded press conglomerates improved the journalists' financial situation, but military censorship has more than ever restricted their freedom of expression.

Sole masters of the freedom of the press, publishers are an unusually conceited group, accustomed to impose their fancy on the country's administrators. Most extract profits from overt or disguised blackmail, promoting their varied enterprises through governmental favors and amassing considerable wealth even when their papers suffer financial troubles or face bankruptcy. Each one of them considers himself an absolute monarch and the recipient of divine revelation. The more powerful they are, the livelier their conceit.

Paulo Bittencourt, owner of the *Correio da Manhã*, for decades the most influential paper in the country, was a bumptious but honest king who used to say that his paper could be bought—but only for twenty cents, at the corner newsstand. Though open to pressure from his business friends and especially from flatterers, he was independent from political groups. The support he brought to the establishment's causes and to foreign investors was ideological and gratis. A highly cultivated survivor of the *belle époque*, in which wealthy Brazilians were brainwashed at Eton and Cambridge and kept cocottes in Parisian luxury, he could barely understand the motives for nationalism. He sided with British and, later, American interests, for he understood their representatives' language and thought their views better than the economic arguments of ungroomed Northeasterners such as Jesus Soares Pereira, the brain behind the push for a state-owned oil monopoly. He had more in common with a Rockefeller or a Rothschild than with the defenders of a country he did not really know. Despite these limitations Paulo was capable of great moral and even physical courage when challenged politically. Niomar, his widow, inherited this courage as well as the paper. Stubborn and frequently irritating, her bravery and loyalty to friends reaches the point of temerity. Nothing short of physical elimination can deter her from a set course. She faces threats, imprisonment, and actual violence with an almost irrational impudence. When convinced of an idea she backs it with all she has. Her strategy allows only for offensives and the unconditional surrender of the enemy.

Two days before the coup the *Correio da Manhã* headlined an editorial calling for Goulart's deposition. Two weeks later, feeling that the country's new masters had little use for the liberal democratic rules she cherished, Niomar Bittencourt had turned full circle and opened her paper to the first outcries of the opposition. Headlong she tackled the great array of political and economic forces that supported the military. So unbalanced were the odds that defeat was spelled even before the battle started. The few months that it lasted, however, marked the intellectual history of Brazil. Driven to the edge of bankruptcy, imprisoned, deprived of political rights, persecuted but never humbled, Niomar Bittencourt can look back and say, as Francis I after the battle of Pavia, *"Tout est perdu fors l'honneur."*

Returning to Rio in April 1964, I plunged into the turmoil of fresh combat with a gusto that left my family perplexed. A conversion is an intuitive burst of truth that is explained only by itself, though it can be imperfectly shared through a slow process of rationalizing. I had been converted into an anti-dictatorship activist during the few days spent in Minas Geraes after the proclamation of the first Institutional Act. I felt as if I could, for the first time, see the true face of my country. And, all around me, among the business relations of the ad agency I was soon to quit, at the clubs and places I still frequented, from reading the joyful statements of the powerful, I sensed the appetite of those who again had Brazil to feast on and were relieved to find their fortunes safely protected by the military. These noises spurred my aversion. I began to look at my class, at my acquaintances, and at some of my relatives with new eyes.

Soon it became clear that our small group of journalists was shifting the *Correio da Manhã* from a simple liberal position to one that defended the nationalistic economic interests the government was hurting. At this point Roberto Campos, Minister of Planning (grand vizier of the Castelo Branco regime and the Brazilian bureaucrat most intimately connected with foreign business interests), invited me for a

Sunday outing on his yacht. He must have felt I could still be co-opted back into the system.

Our group of some twenty people was a selection of up-and-coming young men accompanied by a few bosomy blondes, the type Campos favors. We stopped at a deserted beach to fish and swim. After a while we were joined by the president of Mercedes-Benz of Brazil, arriving in a fast motor-boat. He had flown from São Paulo in his private plane and spotted us from the air. He had reason to know the yacht well: he paid her bills. He boarded, holding a fat briefcase, and for the next couple of hours examined with Campos a pile of documents. Then he downed a gin and tonic, swam and roared away.

The sight of the all-powerful minister dutifully noting the desires of the German industrialist while the promising members of his team went on diving and playing as if there were nothing unusual about this manner of conducting the state's business, was for me a lesson on the nature of the new regime. I realized that indeed this *was* the normal way to use the state as a protector and provider for private interests. It was the way the dominant classes in Brazil had always worked, even during the brief period under Goulart when other groups began to share this access to power and the profits it brought.

One of the most striking traits of Brazilian capitalist development is its dependence on the federal government. Federal favors stimulate foreign investments, industrialization drives, the rise of certain industries and products. The Bank of Brazil is for private enterprise the hen that lays the golden eggs. During decades of unremitting inflation it had provided the São Paulo industrial community with the negative interest loans that assured its expansion and, in later years, even its working capital. Governmental decisions saved the coffee interests from the 1929 crash, bankrolled cattle ranchers and wheat growers in the forties, favored machinery imports in the fifties, and so on. After the economy grew more complex, new umbrellas were provided for the rich through the National Development Bank, the Bank of the Amazon, the Bank of the Northeast and the SUDENE development projects. When an important economic sector failed to develop through private enterprise—either because of insufficient capital, through low profit perspectives or for being contrary to North American strategic interests—the federal government would step in with the necessary investments. In this way it became the sole prospector for oil as well as its main refiner, while the more profitable distribution system remained in private hands. It became also the greatest steel producer, the principal iron-ore exporter and so forth.[1]

The economic might of the federal government is such that it is even enshrined in popular sayings. In Minas Geraes an adage lists the three things against which struggle is useless: water coming downhill, fire going up a slope and the federal government. Everyone knows about the government's influence and also knows whom all these riches profit. But it makes a lot of difference if you analyze a situation learned from a book or if you see this situation unfold under your own eyes on a sunny Sunday morning in the middle of Rio bay. I duly absorbed the yacht trip's lesson of string pulling for personal profit and went back to the newsroom feeling still further alienated from the establishment.

Newsrooms, I feel, are some of the most exciting places in the world. The rhythmically tapping typewriters, the ticking of the teletypes, buzz of words exchanged at different pitches, the telephone bells, the in-and-out rush of reporters, newsboys, and visitors, all create an atmosphere of urgency, intoxicating and unforgettable. Somehow, in the midst of chaos, you learn to concentrate and write. The adaptation is so profound that when you have to work in normally quiet surroundings, the silence distracts you.

[1] Celso Furtado explains in detail how governmental decisions favored foreign and national industrialists after the 1930 revolution, in *The Economic Growth of Brazil* (Berkeley, University of California Press, 1965), the basic text for the study of Brazilian economic history. Werner Baer, in *Industrialization and Economic Development in Brazil* (Homewood, Illinois, Irwin, 1965), and Warren Dean, in *The Industrialization of São Paulo* (Austin, University of Texas Press, 1969) also examine the importance of the state in the development of industrial enterprises in Brazil. Philippe Schmitter goes further and analyzes in great detail the influence of business associations on key economic decisions in *Interest Conflict and Political Change in Brazil* (Stanford University Press, 1971).

Never, as in those early days of May 1964, had I loved the newsroom so intensely, nor felt such relevancy in preparing the next morning's news. We were a fraternal group of half a dozen political editorialists, united by the same ideals and the sense that we stood alone, using to the full the shaky privilege of a freedom of expression that was almost exclusively ours in Brazil. We felt we were the voice of the voiceless. The uniqueness of our work prodded us always to do more, and to do it better. We met daily to decide on the main articles and editorials and we squabbled for the opportunity to write them. Our schedules were punishing but the time would slip away in a wink. Only when we finally dropped into bed just before dawn did we feel our aching bodies and the weight of our fatigue.

Specialists in generalities, as journalists are, we had to fight on many fronts. The new administration was moving swiftly and most of its initiatives called for comments and criticisms. After securing its main constituency by more than doubling the military's pay, it started to implement an economic model aimed at transforming Brazil into a privileged satellite of U.S. business, in a way similar to Canada's. This project called not only for a swarm of extensive favors to foreign investors, but also for a radical reshuffling of the country's administrative machinery and its industrial part. The ESG staff had been convinced by Campos and his team that only by tying tightly to the American economy could Brazil mobilize the excess savings needed for the investments a rapid development rate would demand.

One of the first measures taken by the Castelo Branco administration was to force Congress to repeal the profit remittance law it had approved under Goulart, which had given Brazilian authorities power to control, for the first time in the country's history, profits exported by foreign firms. Then it signed a treaty[2] by which the U.S. government would become the automatic substitute owner of any company the Brazilian government might expropriate for reasons

[2] The treaty the U.S. signed with Brazil is now standard for friendly underdeveloped nations. One of its provisions allows the U.S. government to insure private enterprises abroad.

of public interest. The treaty also made international arbitration committees, not the Brazilian Supreme Court, the final judges of the legality of the Brazilian government's acts, an unheard of assault on the country's sovereignty. It further stated that its provisions were to bind the signers forty years after the treaty is repealed. These concessions, recalling those wrested by the Great Powers from Imperial China or the Platt Amendment of gunboat diplomacy,[3] stirred the first organized protests from nationalistic circles in which, for once, some businessmen stood out. The reason for the protest noises these businessmen were murmuring was another aspect of the policies then enforced. As the ESG-Campos project called for the modernization of industry through mergers and still greater economic concentration, the government stood aloof, shielded by its anti-inflationary plans and the approval of the International Monetary Fund, while hundreds and thousands of slightly obsolescent or overextended firms, large and small, went bankrupt or were swallowed by international corporations for a mess of pottage. These firms faced a credit squeeze on the internal money market. And at the same time exchange facilities were offered to foreign enterprises willing to raise loans on their home markets. Brazilian firms had to sell out or close. By December 16, 1966, *Time* magazine was already reporting that Brazilian companies with good market outlets were up for grabs at 60 per cent of their assets and that foreign investors had gained control of 50 per cent of Brazilian industry since the 1964 coup.[4] This process of denationalizing an economy

[3] The Platt Amendment to the Cuban Constitution was an eight-item clause approved by the U. S. Senate that allowed the United States to intervene in that country in order to set up a government it deemed capable of assuring protection to life, property, and individual freedom. This amendment also provided for American intervention if Cuba did not fulfill its obligations toward international creditors. The legal basis for North American oppression of Cuba, this amendment became a reference point for all Latin American nationalists in their struggle against imperialism.

[4] Some other studies about foreign dominance of Brazil's industries can be found in Eduardo Galeano, "De-Nationalization and Brazilian Industry," *Monthly Review*, December 1969, p. 13; Rubem Medina, *Desnacionalizacao, Crime contra o Brasil?* Rio de Janeiro, ed. Saga, 1970; Celso Furtado, *Dialetica do Desenvolvimento*, Rio

has embarrassing results in middle- and long-term planning because it transfers to other countries—especially the United States—the decision centers of major economic activities.

While the denationalization of the economy was a quiet procedure, invisible except to expert eyes and spread over a considerable period, the social consequences of the anti-inflationary policies with its capital-concentration objectives were highly visible and were felt at once.

The government decided to throw the main burden of its stabilization programs on the wage earners by limiting their raises to less than the inflation rates. This meant that most Brazilians would become poorer and that working class salaries, already low, would quickly fall to mere survival levels. Foreseeing that decreasing revenues and lower standards of living would trigger protests, the government launched a systematic persecution against urban and rural trade unions, justified as usual by the need to purge them of "Communist infiltrators." The Ministry of Labor intervened in the affairs of the bigger unions, replacing the elected officials it had recalled or imprisoned with its own bureaucrats. The most active leaders were stripped of political rights, arrested, or forced into exile. New regulations made it mandatory for candidates to trade union posts to produce "ideological certificates" issued by the political police. Legal strikes became increasingly difficult to organize. Later, strikes were declared a crime against national security. In the Northeast, landowners, policemen, and military started to hunt down leaders of the Peasant Leagues and rural unions, including those supported by the Catholic Church. Many were tortured and killed.

The Brazilian labor movement never had the independent grassroots participation and aggressive militancy of its Argentinian counterpart. Formed under Vargas during the

de Janeiro, Fundo de Cultura, 1964, p. 133 and following; Andrew Gunther Frank, *Capitalism and Underdevelopment in Latin America*, Monthly Review Press, 1967, p. 208–18. The U. S. Department of Commerce publishes statistics on American investments abroad in its monthly *Survey of Current Business* and its periodical *U. S. Business Investments in Foreign Countries*. The United Nations Economic Commission for Latin America publishes annual economic surveys, normally an excellent information source.

thirties, its paternalistic regulations allow for constant official manipulation in the frame of what has been called "artificial corporativism."[5] Dependent on government favor, it failed to mobilize the workers to the defense of their interests. While in Argentina the unions form a strong social backbone and are able to limit the ruling classes' repressive power, in Brazil they are mostly tolerated clubs whose social efficiency depends on the government's will. This lack of organized class consciousness in Brazil is one of the reasons why our military rulers have been able progressively to establish a terrorist state, while those of Argentina are forced periodically to liberalize their policies.

Ever since Vargas, successive populist administrations have tried to co-opt the labor movement through stick-and-carrot tactics which produced for the working class a share of the country's income. After the military take-over, as the former electoral needs of the administrators disappeared, negotiation was replaced by intervention and concession by naked force. The results of these methods are growing disparities in income distribution and a steep increase in labor exploitation.

The minimum wage's buying power had regressed, by 1970, to less than what it had been in 1960. The sixties were a period of uneven development for Brazil, but both industrial output and productivity grew steadily during the decade. The erosion of working class earnings during the decade points to a brutal rhythm of labor exploitation, maintained during the last six years by coercion and blatant oppression. The rich got richer and the poor got poorer, to use an oft-quoted expression from a papal encyclical. This, of course, is happening in most of Latin America, but in Brazil it reaches an outrageous level and is responsible for the regime's growing use of violence.

Fast money has an inebriating smell for capitalists. Owing to the regime's repressive actions, never has money flown faster into the bank accounts of Brazil's investors.[6] But the

[5] Philippe Schmitter, op. cit., p. 112. Schmitter describes with great insight and much precise information the master-servant relations between the Brazilian government and the trade unions.

[6] An example of these excess profits, chosen among many that can be found in the advertising of Brazil's magazines, is a statement

misery and suffering that pays for the profits a few capitalists pump out of the masses is, of course, hardly a solid base for building a nation.

Most historians contend that only those who already have enough to fight for more are efficient actors of revolutions. This common wisdom is based on the crucial role played by the masses of Paris and St. Petersburg during the French and Russian revolutions, a relatively privileged social group in comparison to the peasantry, whose revolutionary ardor was less strong. Now, China's great peasant war and the indomitable resistance of the people of Indochina against French and American invaders have proved that revolutionaries need no more than faith and hope to work miracles. In our modern secular world liberation struggles are similar to the great mystic upheavals of the Middle Ages that welded nomadic tribes into the empires of Islam or transformed illiterate serfs into crusaders and cathedral builders.

The indifference of Brazil's ruling classes and their foreign partners to the plight of those they exploit is encouraged by the thought that the latter are too poor and ignorant to free themselves. This attitude seems rather suicidal, in spite of the duration of some reactionary autocracies in Portugal or Spain. Louis XV might still have had time to wait for the deluge he sensed would come after him. Today, even in an underdeveloped country, history's pace is hastened by immediate communications, by the brushfire propagation of the ideals of justice.

Ideals alone can neither fight nor conquer. They are arms that must be held by organized hands. The process of organizing is long, but it is not unending. And justice and freedom, once tasted, leave a lasting memory in those to whom they are now denied.

In January 1968 I visited the sugar-cane fields south of Recife, the region in Brazil where hunger and exploitation are most brutal. I met a fourteen-year-old boy on a dirt plantation road near Palmares, and gave him a ride. He had already worked six hours cutting cane and was taking his earn-

by a small investment fund, Creasul, that its shares had gained 63.54% during 1970 and 146.28% during the first five months of 1971 (Veja, June 23, 1971, p. 95). These results were not considered extraordinary at the time.

ings to town to buy the family some food. He was illiterate and could not tell me who was the President of Brazil. I asked him if he knew who Miguel Arraes was. Arraes had been the state's governor from 1963 to April 1, 1964, when the military arrested him. He had been the first governor in Brazilian history to order the police not to side automatically with the landowners against the peasants and the first to extend the minimum wage law to sugar-cane workers. This simple administrative measure had transformed the lives of hundreds of thousands of peasants. For the first time they had had enough money to buy beds, and the state's supplies were exhausted the first month the workers were paid according to the law. The second month, transistor radios vanished from the market. My passenger was only ten when all this happened, but I asked him if he had heard Arraes' name.

"Yes, sir," he said.

"And who was he?"

"He was government."

"And why isn't he government any longer?"

"Because he was for the people."

This matter-of-fact answer does not augur well for the regime.

CHAPTER VI

TORTURE

Violence is a rare experience in most of our lives. Torture is an almost unimaginable aberration. Normal people have difficulty believing that some of their fellow men inflict pain and suffering on other human beings as part of their daily routine. When confronted with irrefutable evidence that such monsters do exist among us, we tend to recoil, spreading around our emotions a shield of willed insensibility. When we hear accounts of torture or read the victims' stories, we slip into a defensive mental block. This self-protecting reaction is particularly noticeable in large audiences. Speakers describing torture can retain the public's attention for some time—generally five to ten minutes—but once the audience reaches a summit of indignation, it begins downhill again until it becomes numb and bored. Its anger dies because it ceases to recognize in the torturers fellow human beings.

We react to murder the same way. The individual murder is real. We imagine the wounded body; we identify ourselves with the victim. The knife that strikes our neighbor is also a threat against us. But genocide is an abstraction. When it comes to mass murders, such as the massacre of My-Lai and other Vietnam war crimes, we are unable to personalize the killings and our condemnation becomes intellectualized rather than a gut reaction. Our imagination is left behind and death becomes statistics.

In Brazil, reaction to the constant use of torture against political prisoners has gone from horror to indignation to indifference. Torture is so common that it is now viewed as a fact of life, an unpleasant but unavoidable reality.

After 1969 the government slowly allowed some denunciations, mostly by churchmen, to be printed in order to accustom the public to the idea that "revolutionary terror can only be met by reactionary terror." The official reaction to the first torture documents published abroad was to deny them outright and to denounce them as an international Communist conspiracy against the Brazilian government. Gradually the position changed. Government spokesmen began to admit to "a few excesses, committed by young officers and unauthorized policemen." Finally even the Minister of Education confessed that torture existed. He justified it by claiming it was also a common practice in the countries where the reports were printed, mainly the United States and France. By then most people knew about torture and the official acknowledgment failed to raise protests. Even the Catholic Church, whose priests have sometimes been tortured, didn't react when one of its bishops, Dom Geraldo Sigaud, Archbishop of Diamantina, a leader of the far right and stanch defender of the military regime, said at a press conference in Rome: "It isn't with candy that you can extract information from these people" (meaning the arrested revolutionaries).

The first reports on torture began to leak to the press by mid-May 1964. They started as rumors, as scraps of information. On April 18, DOPS, the political police, issued a note saying that a worker had jumped to his death from the third floor offices of the central police building in Rio. It was later discovered that the man, an ex-leader of the Manaus' shoremen trade union and an alleged Communist, had preferred suicide to more torture. In Recife reporters began to collect frightful tales of suffering as soon as families were admitted to visit their relatives in the overcrowded military prisons. These stories, however, were still too imprecise to draw a pattern. Only on May 26 did a proven case reach the press. A group of students from Rio's Agricultural School, a campus some thirty miles from the city's center, came to the *Correio da Manhã*. They wanted the paper to print how their dorms and classrooms had been invaded by gun-toting soldiers, how a colonel from a nearby army arsenal was running the school, throwing out students and teachers on the basis of anonymous denunciations and how two of the students had been kidnaped in the middle of the night and tortured by a gang of plainclothes policemen and army officers. One of the victims, a frail mulatto boy oddly called Dorremi, was present and showed us the marks he still bore from beatings and electric shocks.

The few dozen students left on the campus had just seen a film about the Mexican-American war and were preparing to go to bed. Dorremi was drinking a cup of milk and talking with his roommate when the door burst open and policemen invaded the room. Arrested, he asked to put his pants on and was taken hands-up to the patio where he was shoved into a car with a classmate, a member of the Catholic Students' Youth movement. He was not afraid. Many teachers and students had been arrested during the previous days and this sort of thing was becoming routine. They were blindfolded and made to stretch on the floor, a machine-gun barrel pointed at their heads. The ride was only a few minutes long. When they stopped the beatings began. The policemen wanted to know where they were hiding the plans for revolution they had allegedly received from Cuba—and the location of the arms caches. Dorremi was unable to speak because his only thoughts were of the blows he was receiving in the dark. He vainly tried to guess where the next one would come from and how he could defend the more vulnerable parts of his body. As he told the story he still trembled with anger and unbelief. After the beating stopped he began to hear the awful guttural shrieks of his colleague, who was getting electric shocks in the next room. When his turn came, he was stripped, strapped to a chair and wires were clipped to his thumb and toe. The wires led to a small box with a turn-handle. Every time it was turned he got a shock and screamed. The pain was in proportion to the speed with which the handle was turned. The ordeal lasted until daybreak. They were finally, still bound and blindfolded, abandoned by the roadside, where later they were picked up by a school car.

Rio's liberal journalists and intellectuals were, at the time, arguing in favor of an ivory tower attitude toward politics and the regime. They had disliked Goulart's weakness but disliked no less—and increasingly—the regime's brutality and its assaults on public freedoms. Disgusted with the populist left, shrinking from the arrogant right, they felt that politicians, military as well as civilians, only tricked intellectuals by having them write speeches in order to manipulate popular emotions. Therefore, they said, let everyone keep to his own field—the politicians politicizing and running the country, the intellectuals intellectualizing and writing their books, painting, composing, teaching, and occasionally getting drunk.

History has shown that intellectuals best fulfill their self-assigned role of critical observers of society when they do not risk their skin. When dissent requires payment in personal freedom, the ranks of the silent and of the approving swell. Only a few stand fast. Their example saves the reputation of a whole generation. So has it been and so it is in Brazil. The advocates of ostrich policies had many followers, and their ranks grew as purges, imprisonment, and torture began to hit the universities and the civil service.

The thin, scarred body of the student incited me to action. I saw in his anguished face the impotence of those who cannot protest when violence is done to them and whose future will hold ever growing brutalities—to be suffered silently. The desire to side with them, that had been slowly forged during the previous weeks, became a resolve. Quixotism may well be the master impulse behind the activism of radical dissenters from a dominant class. At that time, when I had not yet found the rational reasons for action, it drove me to lend my voice to the humbled.

I wrote about Dorremi. I wrote about Dilson Aragão, the first known prisoner to be tortured at the CENIMAR, the Navy's Information Center which later acquired a sinister reputation. I wrote about every torture case I heard of. Soon the *Correio da Manhã* became the end station for an underground communications network that smuggled reports from prisons all over Brazil.

A political prisoner's will power cannot be broken by the bars of tyranny. His cries of rage are not smothered even by the tightest vigilance. He can always find a way to elude his keepers and inform the outside world of his thoughts and sufferings.

We began to receive unidentified callers who would inform us about who was being tortured, where and by whom. We got unsigned scraps of paper, scrawled in haste, with the victims' firsthand accounts of their experiences and those of fellow prisoners. After a while, when the prisoners had overcome their pain and had disciplined their freedom in the jails, they started to send collectively signed statements describing in detail the questioning methods, the instruments of torture, the precise location of the torture rooms, and naming the torturers. Once they drew a plan of the floor of the Navy Ministry where the torture rooms were located, showing its secret entrances. The publication of these drawings caused such a sensation that the Minister considered suing the paper for disclosing military secrets. He was forced to drop the project when it was pointed out to him that such a move would be a public confession of the truthfulness of the torture stories.

Most of the time we could not check the stories we published. They simply rang with truth and the paper took the risk of being hoaxed. Strangely, this never happened. The military never tried to fabricate a trap by which the stories could be discredited.

The battle fought by the *Correio da Manhã* was many-sided, and torture was only one of its aspects. By August 1964, the stories had fallen into a routine. One night, as we sat around the editorial desk discussing what to write for the next edition, I proposed that we should once more concentrate on the issue of torture. That afternoon we had received a letter from an Angolan exile who had been twice tortured by agents of the Portuguese political police at the Navy's torture center. This was a particularly ugly development, for it not only meant that Brazilian authorities were betraying someone who had been granted refuge in our country, but also that they were establishing an international reactionary front with one of the world's most loathsome dictatorships.

The editor-in-chief of our paper was Niomar Bittencourt's son, Antonio Moniz Sodré. He was not a journalist by training and, feeling the economic boycott organized against the paper, his interest was mostly geared to the government's financial and economic policies. Antonio argued against my proposal, saying that the public was by now bored with all the horror stories we were printing. The editorialists sensed a threat and reacted immediately. Otto Maria Carpeaux, who thirty years before had fled Nazi Europe, carrying a dog as his sole possession, turned purple. He is a man capable of apprehending everything with a mind that houses an incredible erudition, but his body is a chaos of uncontrolled movements. Normally he stammers, but this time rage made him speechless. We all ganged up on poor Antonio, reducing his argument to shreds and blowing out all the repressed aggressiveness of our professional relationship. That we should grow weary of torture stories was obviously the government's most cherished daydream. The torturers hoped that public opinion would become hardened to their deeds and thus allow them to go on unchecked. Convinced by our arguments, Antonio generously rallied to the cause. From that night on, the paper's full resources were mobilized for the campaign against torture. Reporters were sent to Bahia, to Minas Geraes, to the South. In Recife, from where the most dreadful accounts came, the small staff pooled information with reporters who worked for papers not so willing to air the facts, but who were personally eager to help our effort.

On September 12, 1964, we were for the first time informed of a death caused by torture. Edmundo Moniz, head of the political staff, got through his military contacts precise information about a sergeant who had died a few weeks after being arrested. He passed it on to me, and the next day a first page article appeared.

Marshal Castelo Branco felt his power threatened by an independent military repressive group and used the occasion to try to control it. He ordered an investigation of the death—the usual bureaucratic way of calling to order unruly subordinates—and sent General Ernesto Geisel, his principal military aide, on a tour of the northeastern barracks. His mission was to stop torture and to bring the local commanders under the authority of the President.

Geisel's trip was a golden opportunity for us to try to contact the prisoners held in Recife, for he asked a group of pro-government civilians to write a report on prison conditions, and their work had to be followed by the press for credibility's sake. At the same time most prisoners—in fact all of those who had been tortured—were transferred to the state penitentiary, the military now considering them a burden.

I decided to follow in Geisel's steps. Just a few weeks before my trip a young reporter from the *Jornal do Brasil* had been arrested and beaten up in Recife. His crime: having written that an officer had been carried away by emotion and had wept at the barracks wedding of Miguel Arraes' elder daughter. This had been considered unflattering to the Armed Forces' virile pride. The reporter told me his story while recovering in Rio and warned me against the torturers' hostility to the press. It was also known that Colonel Bandeira, the espionage chief of Recife, could count upon myriad informers and agents and that he held the city in terror. It would be child's play to stage a street incident and have me beaten or arrested for subversion, a charge that does not call for evidence. Also, it could well be that no one would want to talk, that I would be prevented from seeing the prisoners, that the trip would be a failure and would damage the campaign the paper was waging. I decided to take the risk. Notoriety would be my sole protection, for an assault against the *Correio da Manhã*'s representative would create at the time a national scandal. The day I left, my visit to Recife was announced on the front page.

Cramps of fear gripped my stomach as I climbed the plane's stairway. Often, in moments of danger, I have had this sensation of emptiness in my bowels, a dry mouth and foam-rubber limbs. This is the dread of the unknown, the fright before action. When the crisis actually comes the body and mind concentrate to face it, and the sensation disappears.

I was already calm when I landed in Recife, and I started to look up some of the people on my long list. At first I had a few letdowns with ex-prisoners who threatened to deny everything if I printed their stories. Finally I was picked up by the resistance group responsible for transmitting most of the documents that had reached us. I was passed from car to car in the dead of night. I went from house to house, meeting the prisoners' relatives, filling a notebook with names, dates, medical reports, descriptions of interrogations. The group decided to smuggle me into the prison on a Sunday afternoon when the three thousand common law inmates receive visitors. They checked the guard's schedule and put me through when a friendly policeman was checking and taking down the visitors' names.

Recife's penitentiary is old and overcrowded. Since the state is always in financial straits there is little to pay for the prisoners' keep and they are allowed to sell handicrafts in order to make money for extra food, cigarettes, and marijuana. During visiting days the main patio looks like a marketplace. The prisoners display their carvings, horn and leather articles, pottery, whatever they have made that could be sold. Guards are lost in the crowd and surveillance is half-hearted.

Political prisoners receive their visitors in a smaller but also loosely guarded patio, separated from the main one by a wooden fence. I found perhaps one hundred of them sitting on benches or standing under the shade of some trees talking to their families. My presence, which had been announced, did not disturb their routine. We all tried to act normally and draw as little attention as possible. I stayed at a far corner taking notes behind a curtain of bodies. Everyone who had been tortured—some fifteen or twenty—would come up, tell his story in the most concise and factual way he could, and walk away. Two hours later I had finished my work. It then crossed my mind that it might be harder to leave than to enter. The military would be only too happy to catch me doing something illegal that would hand them a pretext to keep me. But, after a few anguished moments queuing to be searched at the door, I found myself facing the same well-disposed policeman. He nodded slightly and let me out.

Two names occurred in the tales I heard about those who had suffered most: Ivo Valença, an engineer, and Valdyr Ximenes, Miguel Arraes' brother-in-law, who was the head of a state co-operative formed to sell to peasants, at a low price, food and staples such as drugs and clothing. I saw Valença at the prison. His wrists and ankles were still scarred by the ropes used to tie him upside down from the *pau de arara*,[1] for he had been tortured for three consecutive days.

---

[1] The *pau de arara*, literally the parrot's perch, is the standard position in which political prisoners are now questioned in Brazil. The prisoner is made to sit bending forward as if rowing, and his hands are tied to his ankles. They pass a wooden rod under his knees

He received electric shocks, was shut up in a refrigerated chamber and was beaten to a pulp.

At the time I was in Recife, Valdyr Ximenes was still at the military hospital, which could not be entered. I saw him three years later, still a broken and sick man. The military could not torture Miguel Arraes, the true object of their hate, without risking international protests. They turned their rage instead on poor Ximenes, a man of mild temper and moderate political commitments. The co-operatives he ran had, just before the coup, received a large order of overalls to sell to the sugar-cane cutters. The military labeled them "guerrilla uniforms" and Ximenes was tortured to tell where the guerrilla army's guns were hidden. He had two vertebrae and four ribs broken. The shocks he received were so powerful he temporarily lost the feeling in one hand and had large round burns on his wrists. His condition was so poor when he was sent to the army hospital that its director had a doctor examine him and note on a formal document in what state he was admitted.

Horrible as these sufferings may be, the worst torture case in Recife at that time became fully known only in November 1965, a year after it happened. The victim is a five-foot-tall girl called Sonia Montarroyos, then twenty years old and a member of a Trotskyist group. While passing through Rio in search of political asylum in Uruguay, she told me her story.

Sonia was arrested on November 1, 1964, at a place called Prazeres, near Jaboatão, fifty miles from Recife. Taken to the central police station, she spent a night hearing the terrible cries of the tortured. When the morning bureaucratic routines started, she simply walked out of the front door and hid with some friends, in a poor sector of the city. Three nights later she was left alone while her friends went to a film. She began to be haunted by the screams she had heard in the police station. Finally she had a hysterical fit and ran howling into the street. The neighbors called the police and she was arrested again.

---

and, raising him off the floor, they make the rod rest on two separate chairs or tables. While thus hanging, he generally receives electric shocks.

Back at the police station she was given the works. Her escape had called attention to her and now the jailers believed her more important in the Trotskyist organization than she really was. Superintendent Alvaro Costa Lima, a lifelong torturer and Communist-hunter, Major Bismark, a specialist in electric shocks, and Major Dinaldo started to ask details about the group—how many and who they were, where they met, where their guns were hidden. Helped by some detectives they questioned her over and over for hours. Sonia remembered only one face, the round, bald, mustached face of a short man who burned her with his cigar. I saw the scars on her arms and stomach almost a year later. Since she was unable to tell them what they wanted, her boyfriend, a Uruguayan called Pedro, was brought in and then three men raped her in front of him. After that Pedro spilled all he knew, but his confession was not enough to buy his fiancée's freedom.

A few days later Alvaro Costa Lima showed her and her group on TV. While the program was being taped Sonia spit in his face. Right after the TV crew departed she was tortured again, as punishment. Then she was removed to an army barracks, where Major Dinaldo had her hair shaven. She was shifted to cells in half a dozen places. In one of them, an army barracks at a place called Tijipió, she was thrown naked into the "Fernandinho," a nickname for a cage in which she could only squat. The cage was kept in a dark cellar, but every half-hour a floodlight went on, which prevented her sleeping. Sometimes, when they brought her ration of bread and water, the jailers would push her head against the bars, just for fun. After a while, a fortnight, she thinks, still naked and in the "Fernandinho," she was taken to the woods behind the barracks and left there under the rain and the sun. She was so lonely that she longed to see her jailers, just to see a human face. Once a soldier gave her his cloak to protect her from the rain. He was punished.

After a while Sonia began to suffer from hallucinations. She thought she was her own mother, or that she was a prostitute whose child had died. Once she was told that her brother had been arrested and she answered that she had no brother (her mother was an only child). Finally, she was removed to the public asylum where she was kept in a cell with eight other patients, one of whom constantly threatened to strangle her. Released just before Christmas, in January she was arrested again and again sent to the asylum, for no clear reason. In April a lawyer got a habeas corpus for her, but it was not honored by the military authorities. Then in June, through Dom Helder Camara's[2] influence, she was committed to her family's care. In August, again for no precise reason, a military court ordered her arrest but she escaped before the order could be executed, and started her long journey toward safety abroad.

The chief torturer in the Recife area was Colonel Helio Ibiapina, a religious maniac. He thought Brazil could only be purified by a bloodbath and he devoted his energies and considerable power to eradicating the two great sins that he believed were threatening the country's soul: Communism and progressive Catholics, the latter a devil-inspired stain that had contaminated the Church's body and was threatening Western Christian civilization. In June 1964, Ibiapina felt the urge to justify himself and the Army before the Church. He asked Dom Helder Camara to address a meeting of the region's bishops and told them, as one of the bishops later confided to me, that he had never denied the existence of tortures, when confronted by the evidence Monsignor Camara often brought to army headquarters. "Torture is the price we, the Army's old guard, have to pay to keep the young officers in line. If they had their way, you would now be protesting not against bad treatment of prisoners, but against their shooting."

General Geisel's inspection succeeded in stopping torture for the rest of Castelo Branco's term. Since the legal opposition offered no threat to the regime and the armed resistance did not yet exist, it was unnecessary. By mid-'68,

---

[2] Dom Helder Camara, Archbishop of Recife, is one of the Catholic Church's most influential progressive prelates. A spokesman for the Third World's deprived masses and for a Christian commitment to social justice, his voice is widely heard in Europe and the United States. He is a vocal critic of the social policies and tortures of the Brazilian military and is considered one of the regime's worst enemies, though no one has yet dared to imprison or kill him.

however, with students taking to the streets, workers beginning to strike, and the first acts of urban guerrillas being identified as such, the torture started again, on the pretext that only by violence could military intelligence gather the information it needed to defend the state. Since Institutional Act No. 5—issued on December 13, 1968—when all controls on the political police were waived, it has become the routine way for questioning suspects.

The 1969 code for military penal procedure has an opening for a period when torture can easily take place. It allows a prisoner to be kept in absolute seclusion for forty-five days, during which no legal testimony is recorded. This blackout period—which sometimes is extended to more than six months—is used to extract confessions and information. Only later, during the "inquiry" phase of the procedure, are confessions taken down in juridical form.

In Brazil today a person arrested in connection with "subversive" activities—even if only as a witness—stands a better than 80 per cent chance of being tortured. To be hung upside down from the *pau de arara* for half an hour and to receive a few electric shocks is considered a more or less normal treatment. Torture is conducted in well equipped centers such as the OBAN—Operação Bandeirantes—headquarters in São Paulo, or the CODI—Center of Internal Operations—building at Barão de Mesquita Street in Rio. There is, of course, room for some independent initiatives by the political police, the Air Force, and the Navy.[3]

Though even the most innocent-looking object can be used to inflict pain on the human body—an open upturned tin can being as efficient as a knife or a razor if a prisoner is made to stand on it barefooted—torturers have a weakness for gadgets. They favor field telephones for applying electric shocks because the current's intensity can be regulated by the speed with which the handle is cranked. São Paulo's DOPS —Political and Social Order Department—invented a "Dragon's Chair." This is a barber's chair covered with metal strips

---

[3] Torture is today as routine as ever. It may vanish from the international press for a while, but it always pops up again. A lull is sometimes a consequence of a decrease in urban guerrillas.

that can be plugged into the room's electric circuit. Through a hole in the middle the prisoner's testicles are tied to a piece of wood under the table's surface before he is given shocks. The display of imagination also applies to the nicknames given to different tortures: a "Chinese Bath" consists in keeping the victim's head under water almost to the point of drowning; a "Christ Redeemer" in obliging the prisoner to hold telephone books while his arms are outstretched as on the Cross, and so forth.

It is obviously easier to obtain information by means of torture than through cross-examination. Brazil's military have obtained some of their most crucial information in torture chambers. Two racked Dominican priests gave away the password that led to the execution of Carlos Marighela, the most important urban guerrilla leader. Information gained from torture put the police on the trail of Joaquim Câmara Ferreira, torture-murdered in 1970, and of Carlos Iamarca, shot in 1971. Hundreds of other revolutionaries were arrested and many died because their comrades cracked under pain.

It is morally impossible to condemn someone for not resisting torture, but the absence of guilt cannot free the tortured from political responsibility. Brazil's experience shows that if a victim starts to individualize his sufferings and therefore to imagine the possibility of surviving, his will to resist diminishes. Only those able to place their own pain in the context of the general struggle for our country's liberation can, hanging upside down from the parrot's perch, behave as a true representative of the oppressed, and keep mum.

Such behavior is the product of a deep political conviction. Unfortunately urban guerrilla groups have failed in perfecting their members' political preparation, a failure that is dearly paid for when they are confronted by torture.

Death is often the price of silence. A tormented revolutionary may welcome it as a blessing and hope that the excruciatingly slow deliverance may finally free him. The regime considers it a blunder to kill a prisoner during the initial phase of investigations, when he has not yet been squeezed of all he knows. In some centers torturers are assisted by physicians who try to keep the victim alive so that torture may go on. The perverted science of these doctors has not prevented the death roll from climbing steeply.

Virgilio Gomes da Silva, a worker killed under torture in São Paulo on September 29, 1969, was a hero, but at the time also an exception for deaths under torture were then unusual. He exasperated his torturers when answering their questions by saying only that they were going to kill a Brazilian patriot. When they failed to drag information out of him after torturing his wife before him and murdering with electric shocks his four-month-old baby, they let out their fury by bursting his head against the wall. In 1970 the number of murdered prisoners rose and there is evidence that, starting from 1971, the murder of revolutionary leaders has become standard practice.

A policy of murder spares the government the embarrassing intervention of international human rights organizations and avoids the possibility of having to exchange important prisoners for the lives of kidnaped foreign ambassadors. Thus Joaquim Câmara Ferreira, Marighela's successor as head of the ALN guerrilla group; Devanir José de Carvalho, leader of the MRT group; and Eduardo Leite, called Bacuri, of the VPR, were some of the many revolutionaries murdered in prison since October 1970.

Bacuri's death was particularly dramatic. He was captured in July 1970. Tortured at OBAN's headquarters, he was later transferred to an isolated cell at the Tiradentes State Prison where many of São Paulo's political prisoners serve their time. Though he could not be seen, he kept shouting his own name, saying he was alive and that the Death Squadron would murder him. The shouts and his fellow prisoners' protests created such an uproar that Bacuri was removed to the less crowded political police jail in the DOPS building. On October 24 the police told reporters that Bacuri had escaped with Yoshitame Fujimore, a fellow prisoner and also a leader of VPR, as they led the police to the meeting place where Câmara Ferreira was arrested. The announcement amounted to a death sentence. Actually, at DOPS Bacuri had been placed in an entrance cell whose door had been oiled to turn without squeaks when the murderers came for him. According to witnesses Bacuri had both legs broken and an eye pulled out.[4]

When the Swiss ambassador was kidnaped in Rio, the military knew that Bacuri's name would head the ransom list. That night the Death Squadron came for him. He heard them coming and yelled, awakening his fellow prisoners, who started to slam their cell doors. The metallic clanging was his death march. On December 9 the police published a note saying that Bacuri and Fujimore had been slain during a gunfight.

The bodies were left in a small graveyard by the seashore, where Bacuri's mother and wife were able to see them, an unusual procedure, for the military generally hand out corpses in sealed coffins and stand guard to make sure no one will pry up the lid. Bacuri's mouth was gashed from ear to ear. An ear lobe was missing, as well as both his eyes. Denise Crispim, Bacuri's wife, wrote a report on how she found her husband's body when it was handed over for burial.

It did not take long for Brazil's top administrative and military echelons to accept torture as an instrument for controlling the country, for enforcing their economic policies and for keeping the regime going. Soon the repressive agencies started to use it also as a tool for wringing independent power for themselves as well as for terrorizing the population and discouraging attempts to organize opposition.

When a regime's primary concern is its own security, those in charge of insuring it gain untold power. Not only do they acquire a disproportionate influence over the affairs of the state, but also unchallengeable authority over the lives of all citizens. For the political police and their military commanders immense new possibilities for corruption are opened up. Everyone is willing to pay for protection. This readiness is a bottomless treasure for blackmailers. Brazil is today in a situation similar to that of certain small Sicilian villages or to New York precincts controlled by the Mafia. Only it is a "Mafia"-controlled country of one hundred million.

To prove its power and assert its authority over com-

---

[4] Ubiratã de Souza, one of the prisoners exchanged for the Swiss ambassador to Brazil in January 1971, was in a cell next to Bacuri's.

peting military groups, the repressive system has to organize sporadic displays of force. In November 1970, a few days before the government-controlled parliamentary elections, an "Operation Birdcage" was staged all over Brazil. Thousands were arrested: labor and student leaders, professors, lawyers, intellectuals, doctors, priests, people from every walk of life who had in common only some sort of dissent record. The impact of this massive operation in such an interwoven society as Brazil's was, as expected, astounding. Countries with small elites have social interrelations unimaginable in the mass societies of the developed world. There is always someone in a family able to phone a general, a governor, a minister. These contacts make each arrest a personal concern for those in power. From all over the country prisoners' relatives pressured authorities for their release. Their clamor quickly reached Marshal Medici and his ministers. Professional associations, such as the influential lawyers' guilds, protested publicly, and even the intimidated press argued against the abuse.

The hard-line officers who run the repressive apparatus knew that they would only be able to keep their prisoners for a few days. Their purpose in arresting them was strictly political—to state once more the preponderance of security over all other governmental objectives, including any liberalizing policies that might exist. They needed just a short time to drive their point home, and anyway, with jails already jammed with thousands of regular subversive customers, they had nowhere to keep their new charges for long. Information-gathering was a very low priority for the organizers of Operation Birdcage. They could not interrogate such a mob. Some officers, however, decided not to waste the occasion. They made their prisoners undress and hold hands in a circle standing on a wet floor. Electric shocks were given to those nearest. The current ran the circle, impressing on the victims the military's absolute power.

The use of violence and torture as tools to maintain social oppression can be best perceived in the countryside, where the black-and-white contrasts of class rule are not blurred by the complications of city life. Two exemplary cases happened in Maranhão, a region that lies between the flooded deserts of the Amazon and the teeming Northeast.

Maranhão has long been considered an alternative location for land-hungry peasants, for its fertile arable lands are mostly state-owned and cheap land is an essential condition for colonizing schemes. The first SUDENE agricultural projects, in the early sixties, called for the relocation of several hundred thousand Northeasterners to this humid territory. Though they were never fully implemented, a considerable spontaneous migration took place over the years, settling thousands of families on claimed forest land by the roadside. New villages sprang up and old ones mushroomed into wooden towns full of gambling houses and commercial warehouses similar to the gold-rush camps of the American West. As soon as the settlers' rice paddies began to prosper, rich men from the cities flocked back to the interior with their lawyers and policemen, flashing impressive papers full of seals and incomprehensible legal words and claiming that the land was theirs. Conflicts over land ownership developed. In many places the peasants organized to defend their rights. Some, possibly remembering the Peasant League's days in their home states, started co-operatives meant not only to counteract property claims but also to free men from the exploitation of grain dealers and cattle ranchers.

The co-operative of Pindaré Mirim was such a peasant organization. Led by a Northeasterner called Manuel da Conceição, it began to force cattle ranchers to fence in their farms to keep cattle from stepping on and eating the settlers' rice. After warnings, the peasants killed a few oxen they found on their fields. They also rented a truck to sell their rice directly in São Luiz, only two hundred miles away, for a price five times higher than that offered by the dealers, among whom the most prominent was the local mayor. They even started a medical post and a co-operative drugstore.

On July 13, 1968, while a few peasants and their families were queuing in front of the medical post, a police station wagon stopped nearby. Seven men, armed with revolvers and machine guns, stepped out. They called Manuel da Conceição. When he came near he was held fast by three policemen while another fired five shots at his feet. He was

taken to the local prison where he received medical attention only three days later, when some of his toes were already
rotting. Taken to São Luiz the next day he had to have a leg
amputated to stop the gangrene.

At the nearby village of Caroatá, in July 1970, the
federal police arrested fourteen peasants and two priests,
Gabriel Gallai and Lourenço Diniz. The peasants were
beaten, the priests only held. Their crime—organizing a
co-operative and building a first grade school. The peasants
were given a choice, either to stay in prison or to destroy the
school building. They took their pickaxes and tore down the
thin chance they had managed to offer their children to
achieve a better position in life.[5]

The use of force to stop settlers from protecting their
rights to the land they till, to stop the bypassing of greedy
grain dealers or to forbid peasants' children from learning
defines the regime's reactionary nature. But the terrorizing of
workers on strike, the shooting of protesting students, the
imprisonment of progressive clergymen, the torture of revolutionary militants are no less eloquent. In order to survive,
the Brazilian military dictatorship must use all these
methods. It can try to limit wanton acts of violence committed by low-ranking officials, but it cannot give them up
without risk of disintegration. Therefore the many international pressures brought to bear on the government over
tortures inflicted upon political prisoners[6] can be useful in

[5] The Caroatá case was publicly denounced by the region's
fifteen Catholic bishops who were also protesting the arrest and torture of a young Brazilian priest, José Antonio Monteiro, and a
French missionary, Xavier de Maupeou. Signed on August 25, 1970,
the document appeared in Rio's papers on August 29.

[6] Among many institutions that have appealed to the Brazilian
government on behalf of prisoners or that have asked for investigation facilities are: the Geneva-based International Commission of
Jurists, which issued a report on July 22, 1970; the Brussels-based
International Association of Democratic Jurists, which, with the
Catholic Jurists Association and the International League for the
Rights of Man, issued in September 1970 a joint statement on the
findings of a mission to Brazil; Amnesty International, a London-
based group; innumerable workers associations and religious groups,
such as the Vatican's Commission for Justice and Peace, the CLASC,
Latin American Confederation for Christian Trade Unionists, and

some individual cases—indeed it is known that some prisoners' lives were saved by international public opinion movements on their behalf—but they cannot force the regime to banish torture. Only the Brazilians themselves can achieve this, by overthrowing the dictatorship.

---

the World's Federation of Trade Unions. The International Red Cross Committee tried several times—and failed—to be admitted to Brazilian prisons although it gets into prisons nearly everywhere, including South Vietnam. The OAS Commission for Human Rights was also denied facilities to conduct an investigation. The U. S. Department of State twice publicly manifested a mild apprehension over torture reports, on April 21 and July 23, 1970. The U.S. ambassador to Brazil, however, though acknowledging that torture exists, apparently accepts at face value the Brazilian government's assurances that it does not condone it.

CHAPTER VII

DISCOVERING THE WORLD

Torture made me finally see Brazil. I already knew its misery. I had seen its forests and deserts, its rolling pasturelands and the hard edges of Minas Geraes' iron mountains. I had met gold-washers in the Amazon and hungry peasants in the Northeast. I had suffered with them and I had longed to help. But this had been a superficial feeling arising from accidental encounters. It was as if I had been a visitor within my own country, seeing its reality for brief spells and then retreating back to the well-padded indifference that an affluent city life offers even in underdeveloped countries.

Torture not only angered and outraged me, it made deep inroads into my consciousness. It gave me new eyes with which to see the Northeast's misery. It brought me into contact with men and women who unflinchingly face persecution for their beliefs. It introduced me to some of the people who most influenced my political development—members of the AP (Popular Action, a revolutionary movement); priests and laymen committed to help the dispossessed find an end to their plight; workers conscious of their revolutionary mission; teachers and intellectuals who were finding a new destiny for our country by systematically questioning the values they had been taught at ruling-class schools and universities. For the first time I was part of my people, sharing their food, their shelter, their trust and their poverty.

The discovery of torture prodded my doubts and made me search for answers in the writings of men whose doubts had led them to change their lives and opinions, as I was soon to change mine. I was also led to the depths of Christ's message, which I had previously known only in its shallow formal aspects.

Like most Brazilians, I had seen Catholicism as a ritual religion whose function was to preside over the great moments of one's social life, from birth and baptism through marriage to death and burial. I was taught that only through liturgy could one find hope. I was fed a stale set of rules that lacked even the vaguest breath of life, numbered 1 to 2.414 in a book of Canonic Law, written in Latin four hundred years ago by Roman bureaucrats. The dialectic tensions that give meaning to a man's relations with his Savior and that are the essence of our freedom of choice were quite foreign to them. I had never heard of Christ as a path to Himself, a permanent questioner who offers His word as a beacon to our quest, an answer to our riddle. I learned only an individualistic formula in which obedience and chastity were the barter staples for acquiring real estate in Paradise—a deal that didn't particularly attract me. Never had I heard a hint about the living sense of charity.

I rejected this barren code as soon as I could get rid of maternal solicitude and think for myself. As some of us do, I had to discover Christ in my adult years and to bridge the abyss that leads from formal Catholicism to Christianity.

I first visited the Northeast in 1958, during one of the cyclical droughts that every ten years or so catch the government by surprise and leave thousands of peasants wandering the roads in search of food, work or escape. The twelve hundred miles I drove through the scorched lands of Rio Grande do Norte, Paraíba, Pernambuco, and Ceará were a nerve-wracking introduction to horror and impotence. Hunger ceased to be an abstraction. It became a myriad of small children with immense eyes, limbs like sticks and swollen bellies. It was the little cardboard boxes or white hammocks carried to the graveyards with newspaper shrouds, the sullen stares of men and women who squat for hours waiting for nothing, too tired to move.

I wandered from one starving group to another taking notes for my reports. I was also learning how unnecessary starvation is. For many decades the federal government had been building dams in the Northeast, but not a single irrigation ditch led off from the reservoirs. Either no one had thought of expropriating the irrigation basins or no one had dared do it and face the landowners' political revenge. Only in one place had the Ministry of Agriculture tried to put the stored water to work. The oasis it built with public money was used by two or three landowners to raise banana trees—extremely thirsty plants—instead of the staple food crops the ministry's agronomists had suggested planting. Most of these lakes were fenced off by barbed wire with "No Trespassing" and "Fishing Illegal" posted everywhere.

At a place near Curraes Novos, Rio Grande do Norte, I found three or four hundred people clustered round a large shed. They had come there hoping to find an emergency job at a public construction project. Along the road the *xique-xique*, a wild, spokelike cactus, had all been cut down, which told much about these people's hunger, for boiled *xique-xique* can be eaten only at the price of colic and cramps. My map had a blue spot marked "dam" at that place. The official budget report of the government's anti-drought department stated that nearly one hundred thousand dollars had been spent the previous year on building the dam. As it turned out, the "dam" consisted of a ditch a yard deep and two hundred yards long. It was located on land belonging to a federal congressman, later elected to the Senate, a man who supported Kubitschek's administration and every single succeeding administration since, including the military dictatorship.

One had only to look at the site to see that the money had been stolen and that these people were paying with their lives. I almost wept with anger at my inability to help the men and women who crowded around the jeep, asking for food. The most I could do was to photograph the ditch and send a telegram reporting the story and the congressman's name. This didn't fill many stomachs. The telegram was published and its impact lost the next day amid hundreds of similar accounts arriving from all over the Northeast. The congressman defended himself with a speech delivered during the early hours of an empty session, and there the case rested.

The cruel consequences of the Northeast's political corruption filled me with indignation but I was unable to go deeper and examine its causes. I had been trained as a reporter in the American tradition: to transmit facts and to describe situations, never presuming to judge. My role was to be "objective," to present the superficial quantitative value of events, without puzzling over the "whys."

I returned to Rio in frustration. I rejected the dishonest members of the ruling class to which I belonged; at the same time I was not able to identify myself with the hungry and ignorant men and women toward whom my sympathies moved. This ambivalent attitude, the basis of all paternalism, is, I believe, a normal middle-class reaction and one which is certainly shared by many young Brazilians including some of those in the Armed Forces.

All of those concerned with Brazil's destiny are obsessed by the Northeast. We feel the Northeast to be a sphinx at the door of our future. Its terrible poverty is the sum of all our past economic and social scourges. It is a challenge that must be met or it will destroy the rest of the country, spelling out its failure as a historical proposition and as a viable entity. We know that half of Brazil cannot survive in relative prosperity while the other half starves to death. Therefore the region's problems are on the minds both of those who want to save the present capitalist society and of those who want to change it for a socialist one.

The status quo has been defended by successive governments ever since a modernist capitalist outlook began to spread over the administration's bureaucracy in the mid-fifties. All the makeshift solutions a technocrat could invent were tried: huge tax incentives to promote industrialization, creating new jobs; public works and housing projects to absorb unskilled labor; agricultural improvements and well drillings in the dry interior; migrations toward the Amazon and the humid central lands. All failed. The money poured into the region is quickly re-exported back south as profits or goods. Modern industries have in many cases reduced the number of jobs available and, even by optimistic calculations, have offered, at most, 60,000 new opportunities over ten years. In fact the "aid-projects" for the Northeast repeat internally the same distortions brought about internationally by U.S.-AID, Alliance for Progress, and the World Bank. They help the same people—foreign business and local oligarchs—and the result is the same decapitalization of the underdeveloped areas. The only difference is that internally the development pole is São Paulo and the northeastern states are the satellites, while internationally New York is the financial center and the Latin American nations are the satellites.

The only economic incentive technocrats have been unable to use is land reform. For decades they have recommended it as a pain-relieving drug as well as a necessary step toward broadening the nation's consumer market. Even Planning Minister Roberto Campos, a technocrat exceptionally insensitive to social problems, proposed a land distribution scheme in the Northeast as a way to gain time for the South's final economic take-off. Up to now, however, technocrats have lacked the political muscle to push the reform through. Local land oligarchies—especially the sugar interests—have shown a surprising ability to co-opt all attempts against their privileges.

Many socialist analysts hold that no changes are made in land tenure because of a supposedly unshakable alliance between landowners and the urban bourgeoisie. This is an erroneous premise based on a mechanical and static application of Marxist theory. The truth is that a ruling class tries not to commit suicide and always makes the general interests of the system prevail over the conflicting interests of a given sector. In the long run the whole capitalistic structure of Brazil will be threatened by the Northeast's social problems. If that threat is judged to be sufficiently sharp, the industrialists, supported by the military and other urban middle-class groups, will enforce land reform. Meanwhile, as a combination of police brutality and modernizing techniques succeed in keeping the countryside calm and producing, the ruling groups allow their land-owning partners to rescue what they can and to squeeze their peasants in order to accumulate capital to invest in other activities. The timing may be faulty—in which case a peasant uprising can hasten the reform's pace—but the system is, in fact, ready to alter land-tenure institutions in order to survive.

Despite all technocratic projects and the feasibility of a localized agrarian reform, northeastern problems are worse today than a generation ago. Misery and unrest spur revolutionary movements to concentrate much of their effort in the region. In fact the Northeast's explosive potential is so obvious that the rightist military dictatorship has a general staff contingency plan that calls for Brazil's partition into two halves, abandoning the destitute North to a socialist experiment while building up the South into a "bastion for democracy" and capitalism such as the Thieu regime in South Vietnam.

To succeed in Brazil, revolution must conquer the countryside. Even if a Chinese-style peasant war is not waged, even if the military decisions are reached in the cities, even if revolutionary transformations are achieved by urban uprisings, the rural masses must shift their allegiance for the revolution to survive. They must shift from a fatalistic acceptance of the exploiting system to an active armed rejection of it.

Peasants are practical people, who only dream when they sense a real opportunity of making their dreams come true. When they acquire a revolutionary conscience, they go all the way, year after year, generation after generation if need be. In Brazil the peasants must be won to make the countryside secure for the revolutionary forces. Only among the peasants can we find the manpower necessary for a victorious revolution. Only on their land can the revolutionary armies form, train and rest.

If any large peasant group is now ripe for political action in Brazil, it is the sugar-cane field hands on the great plantations of the coast of Paraíba, Pernambuco, and Alagoas. They have many inbred advantages for a revolutionary option. First, they are part of a developed capitalist production unit, whose economic possibilities have slowly decayed. This turns the plantations into immense grinding-machines trying to compensate for the drop in competitiveness on the sugar market by overexploiting their labor force. Work relations in such a situation are necessarily harsh and impersonal. This eliminates the paternalistic relationship that exists in the South's small farms, hindering the political perception of the peasants and masking class conflicts. Secondly, plantations tend to gather many families in villages in order to save on transport and utilities such as water and light. If this makes police vigilance easier, it does the same for political activism and indoctrination, which are normally difficult to carry on among isolated and dispersed peasants of other types of farming. Finally, if plantations are as a rule land-hungry enterprises, a sugar plantation tends to be a land-monopolizing one. When the international price for sugar is high, cane is planted everywhere. In Pernambuco, immediately after the market boom that followed Cuba's exclusion from the American market, I saw cane planted right up against the door of the master's house and between the rails of the seasonally idle railway. The owner lived in Recife, the house being blocked until harvest time, when the first canes cut were those around it. Not an inch of land was allowed for the traditional plots on which peasants raise the corn, rice, chickens, and sometimes pigs that may spell the difference between survival and starvation for their family. This dependence of the peasant upon a monetary market, in which his buying power is exclusively his plantation salary, turns him into a rural proletarian, probably more sensitive to class interest conflicts than when he could count on home-grown food as a non-monetary contribution to his standard of living.

Historically sugar-cane workers are a privileged political target in Brazil. During the late fifties and early sixties they started the first effective rural unions in the country. Helped by city lawyers and organized by political agitators, they had a try at struggling for better conditions and tasted some victories. The Peasant Leagues, of journalistic fame, started as a mutual-aid society for the purchase of coffins at an abandoned sugar plantation prophetically called "Galilee."[1]

[1] Articles, reports, interviews, essays and books on the pre-'64 peasant movements in the Northeast abound. The American government thought they represented a potential guerrilla threat, so funds became generously available to finance academic research on them, much of which was conducted by genuinely liberal and innocent scholars. The best journalistic accounts of the emerging peasant movements are in Antonio Callado's books *Os Industriais da Seca e os Galileus de Pernambuco*, Rio de Janeiro, ed. Civilização Brasileira,

Communists and Catholics competed to start trade unions. Some of the Church-sponsored ones survived the military coup, but these were less aggressive, and had milder political positions. This experience in unionizing forms a basic political fund that can be used by revolutionaries for grassroots organizing.

Memories of happier days for the peasants are especially those of the only time when Pernambuco's government honestly tried to serve the people. Given the state's importance, its influence was felt all over the Northeast. Miguel Arraes' term in office lasted less than two years but it made a profound impression on the peasants' imaginations, as the plantation boy's comments on the road to Palmares show. It was the first time a man from a really poor family held such a key post in Brazilian politics. Before him, a peasant could never dream that someone from the dry-lands of Ceará would become master of the Princesses' Palace, the proud seat of a political power for three centuries monopolized by the country's oldest oligarchy. Arraes' election was a miracle, a miracle that went on working for many months, reflecting on every sector of the state's administration, every corner of its territory and the lives of all its inhabitants.

Suddenly everyone in Pernambuco began playing with letters and learning how to read. For the first time tired and hungry peasants could find a use for reading, since printed words could teach them their rights and what their employers could and could not do. Also for the first time they discovered that if a landowner did something unlawful to them, they could go to the police or to the courts and have their

---

1960, and *Tempos de Arraes*, Rio de Janeiro, José Alvaro, 1964. Francisco Julião, organizer of the Peasant Leagues, wrote *Que São As Ligas Camponesas?*, Rio de Janeiro, ed. Civilização Brasileira, 1962. Another Peasant League organizer, Clodomir Moraes, presents his analysis of the movement in "Peasant Leagues in Brazil," Rodolfo Stavenhagen ed., *Agrarian Problems & Peasant Movements in Latin America*, New York, Anchor Books, 1970, pp. 453–501. Emanuel de Kadt examines the Catholic peasant trade unions in *Catholic Radicals in Brazil*, London, Oxford University Press, 1970, and so does the present author, in "O Cristo do Povo," Rio de Janeiro, ed. Sabia, 1968. Philippe Schmitter (op. cit., pp. 209–12) deals summarily with the subject.

rights re-established. Then, the greatest miracle of all happened: sugar mills were forced to obey labor laws—Sundays off, paid vacations, and overtime pay! The cambão (a feudal practice that consists in forcing a peasant to work gratis two or three days a week in exchange for the family plot around his hut) was abolished. The collective agreement Arraes forced the landowners to sign was a model of down-to-earth peasant wisdom. Extremely detailed, it blocks every loophole employers might think of to cheat their workers. It states the exact measurements for a daily hoeing task, both in meters and in the traditionally employed measurements, allowing for less surface if the ground is rough, and more if it is flat and easy. Cutting tasks were also regulated according to difficulty. On mountain sides, weedy plantations, and unburned fields, daily tasks were smaller. They were measured in bunches of so many canes, the contract providing even for the cane's thickness. Strictly applied it made it impossible to rob the peasants. The peasants themselves had been called to write it and having been robbed for generations they knew precisely what to guard against.

The sugar-cane field hands' contract is probably the most revolutionary document ever devised in Brazil. It was enforced only for a few months. The military and their landowning partners abrogated it immediately after Arraes' overthrow. But it planted a seed of hope not easily suppressed by police violence and military investigations.

Way back in his brain, each peasant has stored the memory of those glorious months of relative plenty and justice. He is biding his time. But he will surely try to revive them as soon as he has an opportunity. Meanwhile he survives as he can, keeping the oral tradition of a day in which he was a citizen equal to all. Several of the "A-to-Z songs" that blind poets sing in marketplaces, telling the stories of heroes and saints, deal with the lives and labors of Miguel Arraes, Francisco Julião and other victims of the regime.

Repression took a heavy toll of the peasantry's leadership. During the weeks that followed the coup, many leaders were killed by the police and the landowners' bodyguards. Headless bodies were left on the road from Recife to João Pessoa. Others, thrown into furnaces, were never found. This was probably the case of Pedro Inacio de Araujo, better known as Pedro Fazendeiro, handed over by the Army to landowners on September 7, 1964. A large number are still in prison, or forbidden to engage in political activities after having served their sentences. A few are in asylums, maddened by torture. Some used their wits to avoid persecution and are now working underground. One of these, José Eduardo, was personally questioned by Colonel Ibiapina, whose elitist mentality places no value on a peasant's intelligence. José Eduardo's lawyer described the dialogue to me:

"Why did you go to Cuba?" the colonel asked.

"Well, because Dr. Julião invited me."

"And why did you accept the invitation?"

"For two main reasons, sir. First, because we were very poor and were always fighting the landowners in court. Dr. Julião was our lawyer and didn't charge anything. I thought that if I refused his invitation he might take offense and would stop helping us. And where were we going to find money to pay a lawyer? But then, I also had another reason, sir. Every time I was weeding the fields or cutting cane and I saw a plane fly up there, pretty, going zoom, zoom, quickly crossing the sky, I would wish I could once fly in one of them. When Dr. Julião invited me to Cuba I thought that my chance of flying had finally come and I didn't want to miss it."

"And did you enjoy your trip?"

"Well, Colonel, to tell you the truth, I didn't like it very much, no sir."

"Why?"

"You know, when you're up there and the plane is going zoom, zoom, sometimes it falls into pits, it drops under you. My stomach was all upset and I was very scared. Plus the fact that I was afraid to get sick all over the gentleman that was sitting next to me."

"Idiot! I'm not asking if you liked the plane trip. I'm asking if you liked Cuba. Did you?"

"Well, Colonel, I can't say I liked it very much neither."

"And why not?"

"You know that all the people down there are foreigners?

They speak in a very strange way, with lots of peculiar words one doesn't understand. I couldn't understand most of the things they told me and I got all confused."

"And what did you see in Cuba?"

"I didn't see nothing, no sir. I only saw some sugar mills, some sugar-cane fields and some people that looked very much like we look here in Pernambuco. Only they were foreigners and I couldn't understand them."

"I know they are foreigners, stupid ass. But didn't you see other things, war preparations for instance?"

"No sir, this thing of war I didn't see, no sir."

"Didn't you see uniformed soldiers with machine guns on the streets?"

"Yes, sir. Soldiers I saw. The streets were full of soldiers, just like here in Recife."

"And didn't you see anti-aircraft guns on the streets, surrounded by sand bags?"

"Yes, sir. I saw a lot of these sand bags. I even stuck a knife into one of them, to see what was in it. It was very nice sand, fine and white, very good sand for whitewashing. They must want to whitewash a lot of houses down there in Cuba, yes sir."

Colonel Ibiapina furiously threw the peasant out of his room. He labeled him a nitwit, too dumb to be a subversive. A few days later José Eduardo was released, never to be caught again. He had been the leader of the Palmares union, the largest in the Northeast.

Leadership among peasants passes quickly from one generation to the next. In most cases the elders recognize their lifetime failure to achieve better living conditions. They are ready to support and trust younger people willing to have a try. In fact, the poor and illiterate field hand in Brazil is, by the confidence he has in his own youth, far less conservative than his educated and prosperous counterpart in Europe or the United States.

Readiness to follow a youthful lead does not mean that peasants are willing to back any young leader. On the contrary. To be effective, a leader must fulfill many requisites, the most essential one being what in political jargon is called "social insertion." Used to nature's leisurely pace, peasants take a long time to pass a definitive favorable judgment on someone and do so only after long daily contact. Very objective in their needs and goals, they want to find in a leader knowledge of their practical problems. These characteristics make it very difficult—almost impossible—for weekend revolutionaries to blaze a lasting mark on the countryside. A student stinks a mile away on a sugar-cane plantation. Not only his face, walk, clothes, color, speech are different, but also his way of thinking. City logic fares badly in the fields. At most, if the urban agitator is able to capture and verbalize a pre-existing disposition, he may stage a successful protest march or a brief localized action. But the organization he builds will lack roots and will fall apart when faced with repression.

Most peasant leagues and trade unions hastily formed during Goulart's last months in office originated in the cities and vanished quickly. In some places the organizing presence of city dwellers could even be traced on a map. Peasant leagues in Paraíba, for instance, ceased to exist a few miles west of Campina Grande where the road's asphalt pavement ends. This is also the limit for sugar-cane plantations, the boundary between the humid coastal lands and the dry interior, where agricultural holdings are smaller and cattle ranches are sparsely populated. But peasant organizations were more affected by the lack of good roads than by changing types of farming. The city-based organizers were unwilling to move inland any further than they could come and go in one day. When repression came, the police did not even bother to close down city-inspired leagues. They simply crumbled as soon as their inspirers fled south or out of the country for safety. Only where leagues had been shaped by the emergence of a true peasant conscience, where they had been born out of conflict and a lived desire for justice, did they survive. These were places like Sapé, Paraíba, where ten thousand field hands followed Elizabeth Teixeira, a mother of ten, whose husband had been murdered on orders from a group of landowners led by her own father; or like Ribeirão, in Pernambuco, where a murderous landowner kindled resistance with the blood of five peasants he slew.

During Miguel Arraes' term in office peasants sometimes

resorted to violence, but strangely, for people terrorized and oppressed for so long, they used it only in self-defense. Whenever conflicts between peasants and landowners resulted in deaths, the peasant dead were bullet-ridden, while those on the landowners' side had machete or sickle gashes. The peasants fought with their working tools, not with weapons. Most conflicts broke out after working hours, when groups of peasants gathered to present a common grievance. The unequal confrontations left many victims on the peasant side, and noteworthily not a single landowner was killed, though some, like the lord of the Estreliana plantation, not only shot peasants but boasted about it. The peasants had absorbed their oppression so deeply that even while rebelling against it they stopped short of physically harming the oppressor himself.

To learn to be free of the many oppressors one carries is a slow educational process. Each man must learn for himself but he can be helped by those who have already discarded a similar oppressor. In Vietnam during the first months of the war against Diem's regime, members of the National Liberation Front had what they called "mothers of guns" system. What few arms they had they employed to disarm government soldiers, the only available arms supply at the time. The same multiplying system must be used for the political training of peasants. A city revolutionary can light lasting fires helping a few peasants to see their oppression and teaching them how to make others see as well. But only the peasants themselves, when they realize that man can actually change the established order of things, are capable of organizing their brothers for an effective struggle.

Paulo Freire holds that if someone learns to recognize objectively the realities among which he lives he is capable of changing the world. Most people are unable to do this. We generally relate to our world uncritically, accepting it as if it was a not-to-be-altered magic reality. To help someone change from a magical to a critical relationship with life is a revolutionary act. It is the goal of teaching, for, as Paulo says: "Pedagogy must make oppression and its causes the interest center of the oppressed and from this reflection will spring the necessary commitment for his struggle for liberation. The pedagogy of the oppressed, one which cannot be developed by the oppressors, is an instrument for this critical discovery—that of the oppressed by themselves and that of the oppressors by the oppressed, as a sign of dehumanization."

Paulo Freire, like all prophets, is a teacher and a revolutionary. He started the most extraordinary educational experience in Brazil's history among the sugar-cane workers of the Recife area. So extraordinary, in fact, that the military threw him in jail as soon as they came to power and later forced him into exile.

I first met Paulo between release and departure. He was, after a few weeks in prison, staying at a small beach house in the middle of the palm groves south of Recife. I came for the torture stories which had brought me to Pernambuco. Paulo had none to tell. He had enjoyed his imprisonment, the first real vacation he had had in many years. His cellmates, old friends of more activist nature, had made him exercise his sedentary muscles daily and he was feeling fit. For the first time he had time to read Guimaraes Rosa's *Grande Sertão, Veredas*, the greatest Brazilian novel of all time and perhaps the only book in our literature really touched by genius.

We sat under the stars and talked about peasants, words, literacy campaigns almost until daybreak. It was my first discovery of someone unruffled by life, as if he had eternity on his hands. I noted that Paulo showed no bitterness toward those who were wrecking his life and his work. As he looked back on his work, the word he used most often was "dialogue": the goal of all his effort. But, at the same time, he balanced what passive meaning the word might have with regard to social change—a necessarily uprooting process—by preaching radicalism as the only way to discover the ultimate foundations for dialogue.

"The radical man, committed to man's liberation, doesn't let himself be trapped into securizing circles in which reality is imprisoned. On the contrary. The more radical he is, the more he places himself inside reality, so that, knowing it better, he can transform it better. He is not afraid to listen and he doesn't fear discovering the world. He doesn't fear being with people nor to start a dialogue with his neighbor from which greater wisdom will result for both. He doesn't feel himself the master of time, the master of men, nor the liberator of the oppressed. He joins them at a given historical period, to fight with them for the liberation of all."

This radical man, Paulo holds, is the opposite of the sectarian who regards as a lie everything that is not in agreement with his own particular truth. Being mythic, sectarianism is irrational and turns reality into something false which, therefore, cannot be transformed. While sectarianism is always castrating through the fanaticism it generates, radicalism is always creative, through the criticism it nourishes. One alienates, the other liberates.

Paulo's method for teaching peasants how to read was presented officially as a mere technique that helped people discover the ways in which sounds and letters relate during a forty-hour course. In fact it was much more. It had the truly subversive virtue of helping people to recognize both the natural and the human—or cultural—environments in which they lived, and of showing how one can communicate with the human and control the natural. One of its fundamental ideas is that contrary to a child, an illiterate adult already has a fully developed mind whose logic is largely unemployed or distorted for lack of rational training. This mind is like a man lost in the forest who sees only the trees nearby. The literate man—a guide rather than a teacher—can help the illiterate discover the way to the mountain top and to the full view of the forest.

Paulo's journeys toward perception had little to do with the mechanical motions teachers traditionally force upon illiterate pupils. They started as a series of identification talks in which the peasants are asked to describe certain situations from drawings projected on a wall. For instance—a man with a bucket near his house. First the peasants discover that there are things in the drawing that are not made by men—the trees, the birds, the clouds—and others which are man-made—the bucket, the house, the clothes. From idea to idea, they discover that culture is man's answer to nature's challenges. Then three drawings of hunters are shown—an Indian and his bow, a civilized man and his gun, a cat running after a rat. The idea of technology is understood by comparing the

effort made by the illiterate Indian and the civilized man
with his gun. The cat stands for a non-rational hunter moved
by instinct but unable to know why he acts. Other pictures
are shown—a flower vase, a cowboy, a shovel, a sugar mill, a
church. The peasants interpret the relation each picture has
to their own lives. A woman summarized the pleasure she
felt with her new learning: "I like talking about all this because I live like this. While I live, I don't see. Now I see how
I live."

The technical part of the method—learning to read—is
reached almost by accident when the "generating words" are
projected on a screen with the pictures, then projected alone
and finally are broken down into syllables with which the
peasants play, slowly finding out how to build new words.[2]
Paulo warns that if the oppressed fails to identify the oppressor he has within himself and pursues a liberating struggle, he tends to become an oppressor. He may want to achieve
full humanity, but life has taught him to see only his masters
—the oppressors—as human. His idea of a new man is individualistic rather than collective and he may instinctively
want to assume the values and manners of the former oppressors. This reaction may be considered a fear of freedom,
a refusal to adopt a new vision and a new life, the abandon-
ment of Utopia. When this happens, social revolution is be-
trayed. It becomes a mere substitution of inhuman oppressors. It may change and broaden the social area from which
oppressors are recruited, but it certainly doesn't change the
nature of oppression. This was the fate of the French Revolution and of the Soviet Revolution, with its bureaucratic
privileges. China, through the massive effort of Mao's cultural revolution, tries to avoid dehumanization by permanently questioning actions and results. Its ambitious goal is

[2] Paulo Freire developed the concept of liberation through the
discovery of reality in *The Pedagogy of the Oppressed*, New York,
Herder & Herder, 1970. His basic educational theories are stated
in *Educação como Prática da Liberdade*, Rio de Janeiro, Editora Paz
e Terra, 1967, the Spanish version of which was published in
Montevideo by Tierra Nueva, 1969. I base this brief description of
his teaching method on Antonio Callado's in *Tempos de Arraes*,
Rio de Janeiro, José Alvaro, 1964, pp. 123–32.

to establish doubt and dissatisfaction as a critical method toward the creation of a Communist society.

Paulo has no pupils, only converts. He kept flashing danger signals to them during the hectic months in which they were agitating among sugar-cane workers by means of the anti-illiteracy campaign. He warned that peasants may want agrarian reform only to become themselves proprietors, oppressors and, if possible, employers of other peasants. If they are not led first to discover their own human dimensions and possibilities within a collective life of sharing, they are useless both for the revolution and for their individual progress. He pointed out the risks of "massification"—a word then in great vogue that stands for brainwashing—if peasants were forced to accept their teachers' ideas instead of discovering their own. This could give them "overseer syndrome." An overseer is almost always harder on his fellow workers than is the actual oppressor—a landowner or an industrialist in whose place he stands.

The ideas of Paulo Freire were also behind the MEB, Popular Education Movement, created by the Catholic Church, basically financed by the federal government and staffed by militants of Catholic Youth Movements, many of whom were also members of the AP, Ação Popular.

MEB was the only nationwide effort really to educate peasant masses ever attempted in Brazil. It regarded its task as not only to teach reading and writing but to "conscientize" people to their own realities, those of their neighbors and their region. Its program taught them how to know the main social, economic, political, and religious institutions in their particular area and the relations between them. It also taught group work, basic social legislation, and rudimentary ideas about trade unions and co-operatives.

MEB worked through radio schools formed around a radio set and working under the guidance of a local leader—himself generally almost illiterate—according to educational programs broadcast from a regional center. Though a grassroots organization it had a national co-ordinating committee, and state and regional offices. The latter two were responsible for broadcasting, the supervision of schools and the opening of new ones. Operations were concentrated on the most underdeveloped parts of the country, where the peasants' plight was hardest and the social tensions most explosive.

To start a school an "animation" group would visit a village or a plantation a few times, generally after being introduced by a local priest or a peasant already in contact with a league or a union. Meetings would be held to explain the program and stimulate enough community interest to form a class. Then a natural leader would be selected to be responsible for the radio set and the maintenance of links with the regional office. Sometimes these leaders would take on greater responsibilities after training courses at the region's central base. When the pupils, classroom, and leader were ready, they would start to follow daily broadcasts and to send back the results of their work. Contact was kept through letters and visits from the "animation" teams.

Paulo Freire's ideas about individual freedom, non-directiveness, and the need for each person to identify and kill its introjected oppressor kept many of MEB's people from proselytizing too openly. But the temptation was too strong to resist for the militants of revolutionary organizations, especially the AP, that worked with MEB and whose urban student and Catholic origins were already making them feel an idealized fascination for peasants. MEB was an open-minded, nationally established organization willing to guarantee its members full freedom of thought and expression; it was supported by the Catholic Church and could tap century-old magic influence, normally used to favor the dominant classes; it worked exclusively with peasants and had communitarian goals. How—and indeed why—would a young revolutionary refrain from using all this for politically organizing the masses?

MEB's work helped form peasant unions throughout the Northeast. In some places, as happened at a small town of Alagoas, the "animators" encouraged the union to put up a candidate for the city council elections. Traditionally these posts were filled by landowners, lawyers, merchants and other members of the local bourgeoisie. A peasant had never been elected. The union decided to change this and called for volunteer candidates. Several presented themselves, but as only one could run, primary elections were organized. A meet-

ing was held at the main square. The candidates, after ad-
dressing their colleagues, stood in line with geometric shapes
—a ball, a square, or a triangle—hanging around their necks
so that the illiterates, who formed the meeting's majority,
could also vote. As Brazilian law gives voting franchise only
to literates, this was the first really democratic election ever
held in the country. The result was a rehearsal of what might
have happened in Brazilian electoral politics—the peasant
candidate pooled more votes than all the others together.
Before the example could spread the military stepped in, disbanded the unions and ultimately turned elections even for
minor municipal posts into a farce.

As persecution mounted, MEB's organizers became more
and more non-directive. Several regional offices were searched
by the police; many co-ordinators were imprisoned; broadcasts were censored; and all work was closely watched by the
military information services and secret police. The people
who chose to stay and see what could be salvaged gathered
around MEB's national secretary. Methods were changed,
messages diluted, and even the geographic focus was switched
from the politically explosive Northeast to the vast deserts of
the Amazon basin. "Animators" became less and less willing
to suggest critical analysis to the peasants. They gave up not
only the old proselytizing habits Paulo Freire might condemn
as an unwilling oppression, but they even refused to set the
guidelines from which political conscientization could develop. Futile discussions about how to keep groups from being
manipulated by teachers bogged the project down. Slowly
what had been a promise began to shrink. By the time the
government finally shut off financing, other resources could
not be found. MEB began to disappear after its spirit had
long been dead. What was a pilot project of immense value
for educational programs all over the Third World is now
reduced to a few reports, some files and the memories of those
who shaped its adventure.[3]

Two days after our nightlong talk in Recife, Paulo Freire
was in Rio answering unending stupid questions by the

[3] A detailed and perceptive description of MEB's work and
structure is found in Emanuel de Kadt's excellent *Catholic Radicals
in Brazil*, London, Oxford University Press, 1970, pp. 122–59.

colonel in charge of the anti-subversive investigations at the Ministry of Education. He was preceded by a report, signed by Colonel Ibiapina, in which he was labeled a Communist and "an absolute ignoramus."

Paulo had enjoyed all the rest and reading he cared to take during his stay in jail and sensed that even if let free he could not pursue his work and research in Brazil. He decided to ask for political asylum at the Bolivian embassy and see if his talents could serve somewhere else in Latin America. A few months later he was organizing the popular education efforts of Eduardo Frei's government in Chile. Paulo de Tarso, a Christian Democratic congressman who had been Brazil's most dynamic Minister of Education, also went into exile and helped Frei's agrarian reform program, at the time still full of promise. Darcy Ribeiro, the anthropologist, one of Latin America's most original thinkers and the founder of the University of Brasília, the country's only modern university, had flown with Goulart to Uruguay. Soon he was laying out plans for reforming the University of Montevideo and, in 1969, after paying with a ten-month imprisonment for a tentative return to Brazil, he was doing the same for the University of Caracas. Celso Furtado, Brazil's most distinguished economist, taught first at Yale then at the Sorbonne. He is one of the few foreign full professors in a country that pushed academic chauvinism to the point of refusing Einstein a teaching post because he couldn't produce a French degree.

Brain-drain is one of the Third World's worst human problems. Our country's meager resources are insufficient to produce all the highly skilled professionals needed for our economic take-off and to fill the technological gap that is forever widening between us and the developed world. We send students abroad and make huge investments in universities. When, after years of costly study, professionals are finally formed, the best are offered salaries, working conditions, and research facilities in the developed world far better than they could find at home. If they are not politically motivated, if they don't sense that their knowledge is part of their people's common fund for progress, they accept expatriation. As their numbers grow they become an important contribution the poor of this world offer to the rich countries. Once political repression is added to the permanent economic and cultural temptations, the brain-drain becomes catastrophic.

This has been happening in Brazil since the military take-over. Ideological purges deprived our universities of some of their best professors. Most found teaching positions in the United States, France, Switzerland, Chile, even in Israel. Whole scientific areas were crippled, especially in the human sciences. There is scarcely a competent sociologist, political scientist, historian, or anthropologist teaching in Brazil today. But biologists, nuclear physicists, psychiatrists, engineers, and architects were also expelled. Those who chose to stay despite the regime's teaching ban have a hard time making a living, are often kept from publishing and face constant police harassment.

An example: a world-famous sociologist was arrested early in 1971. Kept in solitary confinement at an army barracks for several weeks, he was released without being questioned. No accusations were formalized against him, nor explanations given for his arrest. As he was being shown out of the prison, an officer told him:

"We are sorry, Professor. Your arrest was a mistake. You were not to be arrested until next month."

The witch-hunt at the universities has messed up the lives and work of many competent persons. However sad their individual fates may be, the consequences for Brazil's future are sadder. Deliberate mediocrity in a country's higher education wastes a whole generation. More important—it wastes time, and time wasted fortifies one's dependence, and perpetuates underdevelopment.

CHAPTER VIII

REVOLUTIONARY ORGANIZATIONS

Isa Brisa. Isa Guerra. Guerra means war and it is her real name. It suited her perfectly when we first met, early in 1965. Isa waged permanent war against a military regime that was destroying her dreams of love and justice. By incredible will power she transformed her almost transparent five-foot frame into a permanent-motion machine. She ran from *favelas* to student meetings to semi-deserted trade unions weaving the underground network of AP (Ação Popular) in Rio. She never stopped to rest, but somehow she always gave an impression of calm, as if she had all the time in the world to devote to those with whom she was speaking.

"Little Roughneck," the jailers called Isa during her six-month imprisonment, in which they failed to break her spirit. Rough and thorny she was to those she hated as well as to those she loved—when they resisted or disappointed her. Most of the time, however, she was Isa Brisa for her friends, a constant warm breeze of compassion, encouragement, and comradeship. Her constant laughter squeezed her sparkling eyes to slits, giving her an oriental look. Her enthusiasm moved the most apathetic groups to action. It was as if she were able to discover a good side to everyone and to tap one's last sparks of energy.

Isa was always ready to perform the tasks of resistance and the duties of friendship. Resistance, when we met, meant mostly smuggling people from place to place, collecting information, mending broken contacts and taking part in endless discussions about the failures of populist politics and its future chances. Leftist Brazilian students and intellectuals are a chatty bunch. The frustrations caused by the military dictatorship spurred their normally loquacious tendency to a frenzy before it was dried up by fear.

Isa was an ex-member of JUC—a Catholic Student Youth—from the Northeast. Trained as a social worker, she had been the chief organizer of the Ministry of Education's popular education program during Goulart's last months in office, a project designed to bring students, workers, and peasants together, to learn the conditions of the country. She was also an influential member of AP's inner circle. Contrary to many middle-class revolutionaries for whom "people" is an abstract noun, she knew well the faces of those to whom she committed her life. She had lived and worked for over a year with the poorest prostitutes of the poorest shantytowns of João Pessoa, itself one of Brazil's poorest state capitals. The misery and exploitation she saw developed in her a deep sense of belonging, a radical loyalty toward the dispossessed. It also kindled in her a lasting enmity against a system that bred such inhumanity.

Isa was arrested in June 1964, by the CENIMAR, the Navy's information service. At that time this agency shared with DOPS, the political police, the reputation of keeping the only two jails where political prisoners were tortured in Rio. Torture was then something new. Some officers kept to the same chivalrous code that made a German officer tell the wounded André Malraux, "The Wermacht doesn't torture." A few were already on the path that would later produce a generation of henchmen, but most still shrank from committing such an ungallant act as beating a girl. So Isa was not physically harmed, but the treatment she met was perhaps as bad as actual pain. She was kept for several weeks in a small locker room next to the torture center. The victims' screams prevented her from sleeping at night and she couldn't rest during the day because the room was often used by the Ministry's bureaucratic personnel. Her fiancé, Cosme, had been arrested and tortured. After both were transferred to an island prison on Rio's bay, we began to get reports on the fierce resistance they were organizing against their jailers. Isa and Cosme led their fellow prisoners to fight for their rights. Despite solitary confinement and harsh treatment, they kept their morale high, smuggled out torture reports, established a prisoner's government to represent all in their dealings with the jailers, enforced a daily schedule of exercise, debates, games and rest. Soon they became a symbol of Brazil's persecuted youth, a proof that prison bars are powerless against free people.

Religious history is based on the survival of victims. Christ's example is far from unique. Political history is also full of the victories of the defeated. A naked fakir was able to bind the proudest empire to his fate and slowly build his country's independence from his many jails, as Gandhi did. Dietrich Bonhoeffer, a man marked to die the miserable death Nazism reserved for its foes, could pass from his cell a lasting judgment on his executioners, his country, and his Church. Who were the men who fired on Garcia Lorca's face? Who pulled the trigger that finished and started Che Guevara's adventure? Who sentenced Daniel Berrigan? The names of these people, all of whom held absolute power over their fellow men, are unknown, are lost. But the death of the poet, the murder of the revolutionary and the imprisonment of the priest inspire unnumbered armies in their battle against dehumanizing realities.

In the days that marked Brazil's first steps toward rule by terror all felt the need for an act of defiance that would oppose the plunge into legalized brutality. A young couple, bound by love and their sense of mission, facing up to their jailers, held the emotional weight necessary for a *cause célèbre*.

The few journalists who still voiced criticism and hope began to write about Isa and Cosme. As soon as we began to stir some interest, to draw the lessons from their examples, Isa was moved to a women's prison and, a few weeks later, to a convent. Marshal Castelo Branco's government was more intelligent than its introverted successors, who care little for national and international public opinion. The country's keenest conservative intellectuals counseled the government and their advice was heeded. They quickly saw the drawbacks of allowing the rise to fame of prisoners of conscience.

Isa's release pending judgment, in September 1964, possibly deprived Brazil of an Angela Davis case, but it provided me with a perfect guide to political ideas that were to change the attitudes of many young middle-class people as well as my own life. It also gave me a dear friend and a biting critic, two great assets for anyone, but an invaluable treasure for someone in the political limelight.

Ação Popular was formed in 1961, as a political answer to the need for social commitment felt by Catholic students, professionals and priests. It was non-confessional from the beginning and open to alliances with other anti-capitalist and anti-imperialist forces, a definition that at first meant a common front with the Communist Party and Trotskyist groups in student politics. Its beliefs, as they stood in 1964, were humanistic and rather ill-defined. "Our only commitment is to the Brazilian man," the 1963 basic document stated. "The man who is born under the shadow of a premature death. Who lives with hunger in his miserable hut and moves through life without hope or goal. Who grows illiterate and brutish, exiled from the benefits of culture, of creative possibilities, of the authentically human paths of real freedom. Who dies an animal's anonymous death on the hard ground of his misery." This declaration of principles was based upon some more objective though no less rhetorical analysis. AP rejected capitalism and neo-capitalism, envisioning socialism as the sole just way of organizing society. It considered the Third World's role essential for the defeat of global oppression and exploitation. It criticized the bureaucratic distortions of European socialist nations and saw state capitalism as evil not for its centralized ownership of the means of production, which it favored, but for the monopoly of decision power by a small group not motivated exclusively by collective interests.

Casting these principles into programs and actions in Brazil meant that AP had to abandon the purely nationalistic politics of the past in favor of class struggle and socialist mobilization. Taken to an extreme degree, this line implied the denunciation of agrarian and other structural reforms as bourgeois tricks supported by American imperialism to maintain a modern neo-capitalistic society in Brazil. Finally, as is always the case when middle-class intellectuals try to start revolutionary movements, top priority was given to implanting the organization among peasants and workers. All these principles were expanded in internal documents and remained the organization's guidelines for several years.[4]

AP's political vision was influenced by the concept of an historical consciousness that should result from a critical reflection on contradictions, conflicts, and other aspects of reality—as much as on man's hopes and ideals. A perception of history's evolution should lead to the transformation of the world, and this transformation should be based on an understanding of the real conditions found here and now—*hic et nunc*, a Latin expression which JUC's chaplains taught its militants—and should aim at humanizing the world so as to allow "man, in his freedom and in his action to shoulder the destiny of creation."[5]

Basically, AP's importance in Brazil was its original area of influence. It offered a radical and revolutionary option to those who, because of religious conviction or simply out of prejudice, refused Marxist-Leninism. AP was the bridge Catholics could cross toward socialism. It was a door open to students and peasants scared and brainwashed by years of anti-Marxist propaganda. It was a link between forces historically apart, one on the side of oppression and the other committed to a deep change in society. Unfortunately AP's leadership decided, around 1966, to declare itself Maoist, as if a country with some fourteen or fifteen different Marxist-Leninist factions—including a Maoist one—needed still another. This choice, though it may have satisfied the anxieties of middle-class militants for revolutionary purity, produced splits, purges, and general disarray.

Isa Guerra introduced me to AP's political writings and to some of its leaders in the Rio area. Together they made me see the ambiguity of a liberal position, the futility of fighting effects without facing their causes. They moved me to read again, and in a new light, Marx's basic texts and to

[4] The summing up of AP's positions presented here is based on its *Documento Base*, Salvador, Imprensa Baiana de Economia, 1963.

[5] Henrique de Lima Vaz, S.J., "Consciência e Responsabilidade Histórica," in Herbert José de Souza and others, *Cristianismo Hoje* Rio de Janeiro, Editora Universitaria, 1962, one of the first books to present the views of AP's founders.

study Marxist analysis of Brazil's problems and structure. My reading and the discussions I took part in convinced me that only a socialist regime can make an honest try at solving our problems and at developing our resources for the people's benefit. Capitalism can at most do patchwork. It is unable to free Brazil from its dependence on the United States and, to a lesser degree, Western Europe. Its continued prevalence means the permanent plunder of our human and material resources as well as the progressive marginalization of the population's poorer sectors.

Faced by the new realities of military dictatorship and open U.S. intervention in public administration, many Brazilians were at the time arriving at the same conclusions. What Goulart and Brizola's rhetoric had failed to do, facts were accomplishing. Brazil's socialist movements were finding under stress who were their true militants. Sudden illegality and repression disrupted many efforts, broke up many organizations, but these ordeals dispelled old illusions about achieving revolutionary transformations by following a line of least resistance.

Easy times were over. The opportunists, who had turned left, hoping for good jobs in federal agencies or aiming at an expedient political career, were seeking to buy their way back into the establishment by doing public penance for their sins. João Pinheiro Neto, boss of the Agrarian Reform Authority and once considered radical to the point of having his life threatened by landowners, showed the way. In a letter written from prison he stated that having been a minister before his thirty-fifth birthday, he had already tasted the best that public office could offer and was, therefore, retiring from politics. Many of Goulart's cronies followed this lead. The government, of course, jumped at the opportunity to discredit the Left by publicizing such statements, but the Left itself gained by separating the wheat from the chaff. Its ranks had been swollen by populist featherbedding; repression had reduced it to a core of well-prepared militants. Now these could organize again along sounder lines.

Students and young professionals were the first to react and have since kept up a gallant, though sometimes suicidal, resistance. They were part of a class that had always formed

Brazil's political opinion and they knew that change emerges from action: *their* action, so they thought. AP's largest backing came from these groups. They had formed the organization, developed it into a leading force in university politics and were alone in grasping the complicated ideological jargon of its documents and alone in arguing distinctions between various forms of socialism in order to carve out an area of originality. Despite "proletarianizing" orders and contacts made through MEB and other Catholic movements, the leadership and the main following were still middle-class.

In all Latin American countries students play an important role as a vanguard against the prevailing social order. Their access to knowledge opens their eyes to the workings of colonialism and the extent to which their countries are exploited. This discovery is a common springboard for a revolutionary commitment. The dreary state of learning institutions inspires students with a sense of frustration and uselessness. Classes are crowded, the teaching bad, courses irrelevant, and labs and libraries outdated and inefficient. Students are not given a voice in university policies, and there is no dialogue. In many fields, especially in law and the human sciences, lack of jobs make a college education useless for those who seek to better their standard of living, for the students know that they will not be able to find employment for their skills.

Political conscience and personal frustrations push students to take on revolutionary tasks with the full force of their generosity. They throw themselves into political battles with painful intensity and haste. The humble, anonymous patience and demanding tasks of grass-roots organizing are often too slow for them. They long for immediate results. Normally they favor either the organizations they themselves set up or those that stress activism and immediate tactics. Thus they become the soldiers of the urban guerrillas, the sparks that ignite street riots and unruly demonstrations. Death isn't part of their brief living experience so their unconscious impression of invulnerability leads them to daring follies.

The May '68 student riots that scared the wits out of France's bourgeoisie are almost weekly happenings in Latin

America. The University of Venezuela, once a sanctuary for various guerrilla groups, is permanently surrounded by police detachments and sometimes by tanks. In Argentina, students have united with workers to stage in Córdoba, Rosario, and other inland cities some of the liveliest riots anywhere. The bullet-ridden façade of La Paz University bears witness to many confrontations between students and military strongmen.

Brazil is no exception. The pre-1964 revolutionary rhetoric and mild demonstrations became organized underground structures, with UNE, the National Students Union, which the military outlawed, serving as the engine.

Brazil's political quarrels are reproduced in the deformed mirrors of student politics. In the university greenhouse ideological differences grow like wild weeds, producing unending splits between parties and movements. Abstract notions replace real problems. Disagreement over the phrasing of an analytical document or differences over tactical plans are enough to give birth to new political tribes, each convinced of being in sole possession of the whole truth and of the keys to revolution. In this fragmented world a larger unit such as AP had little trouble in rapidly asserting leadership. In spite of its own divisions the organization has been able to keep control of UNE up to now.

The cornerstones for reorganizing underground student movements after 1964 were the Communist Party Youth and JUC, Catholic University Youth. When the military took over, repressive policies, academic frustration and pro-American governmental decisions helped radicalize the universities. Many students who had never felt concerned with UNE stuck by it when it was outlawed. The few who played the government's co-option game and worked with the organizations it sought to establish were quickly disavowed by their colleagues and forced to quit. Communist and Catholics pooled resources to form a network of student councils all over the country. They jointly bombarded the apolitical majority of their classmates with propaganda and indoctrination.

They organized conferences, printed papers, started systematic discussions of Brazil's problems. Student political awareness grew rapidly. UNE's annual meetings, once a political exercise for a handful of militants, became a mass event. Every classroom elected its representatives, discussed the agenda and voted on the proposed resolutions. Banned and hunted by the political police, the meetings were held anyway—in a basement of the Franciscan convent in Belo Horizonte, at the retreat of American Benedictine monks near São Paulo. Beating police vigilance became a popular youthful sport up to 1968, when the police rendered impotent at one stroke most of the student leadership, arresting 800 leaders in Ibiuna, where UNE was meeting. Just as the first successful holdups and kidnapings infused urban guerrilla groups with a daredevil attitude that was later to claim a high price, the ability to fool the police at this stage of its antisubversion efforts gave students a self-confidence that was also to have disastrous results when the struggle began in earnest.

The buildup of student opposition to the regime marked the growing breach between the technocrat/military administration and the urban middle classes. By early 1967 the radicalized students were already the most visible and powerful part of the opposition. With adolescent fervor their leadership courted battles they were unprepared to face. Competing political groups outdid each other in demonstrations of revolutionary zeal. Sometimes they acted as if the revolution itself mattered less than their own revolutionary pride. As is often the case with groups evolving inside a circle cut off from society, their policies dealt more with the power contest within the student community than with the strategic goals of a long term national confrontation. Instead of placing student politics in the perspective of a larger political chessboard, they played the reverse game, using national politics to influence student disputes. Protest marches, rallies, and sit-ins were organized at short intervals, appealing to a dwindling number of militants.

Students groups would have probably run out of energy and followers had it not been for a police provocation. On March 28, 1968, students were preparing for a demonstration against the dilapidated state of the government-run restaurant where they got meals cheaply. They were surrounded by Rio's military police, beaten, gassed, and shot at.

An eighteen-year-old boy was killed. His half-naked body was paraded through downtown Rio and mourned in the state assembly. Attended by several thousand people, the wake was the occasion for fiery speeches and the start of several months of street fighting all over Brazil.

Student demonstrations paralyzed most state capitals several days each month, and their bloody repression mobilized middle-class public opinion against the government. Once more, young revolutionaries entered an escalating series of demonstrations that again had little to do with the existing correlation of forces or the ability of the masses to strike back. Students took control of the opposition's tactics by presenting to other groups decisions taken solely among themselves on a take-it-or-leave-it basis. They thought no one would risk letting a demonstration or rally flop because a fiasco would reflect on the opposition as a whole, not just on its student branch. Successive demonstrations exhausted the public's sympathy; all were tiring of the too frequent disruption of traffic. Demonstrations began to be called for their own sake, without planning. Even the more committed liberals, those who had always supported the students and were counted on to influence some military groups toward democratic openings, grew weary. Students failed to exploit tactical victories. On June 26, 1968, 100,000 people marched through Rio de Janeiro to protest the brutal way in which a few days before students had been herded into a football field next to the university and beaten. This massive expression of middle-class dissent impressed many officers who had to face their own families' rebukes. For a short while the government, feeling the changing mood of its base, showed a certain willingness to negotiate. The gains that might then have been won were wasted by the students' arrogance and refusal to parley. They believed power was around the corner. After a military coup, a student coup!

Student politics are ephemeral by definition, and in this lies the difficulty of combining with other groups. Because workers often see in students tomorrow's bosses, or fear their kamikaze tactics, because they view students as a passing phenomenon, not a class, workers normally reject contacts with them. The worker-student alliance of oratory fame *can* be set up, but only under working-class leadership and for working-class interests. Students, intellectuals, and middle-class professionals can share in the alliance's leadership, but they will weaken and split it if they try to make of it an instrument for bourgeois struggles or intellectual objectives.

The tactics and leadership of Brazil's student movement prevented the birth, in 1968, of a revolutionary alliance that might have imperiled the regime. Since they involved only the urban middle classes, the conflict's explosive political potential vanished. The military was free to use its huge material advantage. Their power was never at stake, nor was there doubt that the rebellious youth would be quashed before they became revolutionary menaces.

From an immediatist point of view the students' reaction could be considered a dead loss. Too many leaders were arrested, too little was accomplished. Divisions among socialist groups deepened instead of mending by common effort. Results, however, are not so easily judged. Wanton repressive practices during this period have alienated for a long time the allegiance of the young elite. The military leaders will need this elite for running the country according to their technocratic schemes. It is true that many rebel students can be co-opted back into the system by high salaries or access to decision making; or they can return to it simply through despair or the political vacillations so characteristic of the middle class. But even these will lack the enthusiasm which is needed for the development and consolidation of a totalitarian regime.

On the other hand, the era of rebellion persuaded many men and women who normally would not have been politicized to devote themselves to the cause of revolution. Knowledge of the basic rules for underground organizing became widespread. People gradually learned not to brag or talk idly, to inquire only about what they need to know to carry out their tasks, to memorize things that must not be written—phone numbers, addresses, etc. Indiscretion and frivolity are still rampant among young militants, but the toll they take is far smaller than one would imagine with such an experienced movement. The new revolutionaries also learned how to be punctual, how to set up appointments and contact points, how to use a password. These seemingly minor skills can spell the survival of a militant and even of a whole organization. In short, the seeds of future resistance were sown during those years. Soldiers of the forming urban guerrilla groups were perpared then, while other militants became convinced of the revolutionary virtues of patience and well-performed humble daily tasks.

Although political self-discipline has improved, political analysis has not. We are still plagued by the repetition of slogans and mechanically applied schema imported from different contexts. When used as the theoretical base for revolutionary praxis, these schema lead to blunders and failures. The situation, however, has changed since the days when an orthodox Communist bureaucracy appeared as the sole dispenser of revolutionary truth in Brazil. On the whole the Left's empirical knowledge of the country increased considerably with the shift in allegiance of previously conservative sectors, especially in the universities and the Catholic Church. There are indications today that a revolutionary theory adapted to Brazil is taking shape, and will before long guide revolutionary practice. This is an essential development for the future. History shows that a revolution must, if it is to succeed, be firmly anchored in the masses and must appeal to their real needs. Therefore a transplanted model—be it Russian, Cuban or Chinese—always fails.

One of the reasons for the failure of these transplants is their fundamentally anti-Marxist nature. Perhaps Marx's greatest single contribution to political thought was the introduction of the concept of change to the scientific analysis of social relations. If one freezes a Marxist analysis in time and space and tries to apply this dead model in another country at a different epoch, he disowns a basic truth of the theory he believes in. Strangely, this has been precisely the behavior of many of Brazil's Communist parties and groups. In the name of fidelity to Marxism, they forget Marx's lessons of history, just as most Christian institutions deny Jesus' teachings in the name of orthodoxy. Lenin gained power because he was the best analyst of the changing political conditions in tsarist Russia; Fidel and Che took Havana because they developed the most efficient tactics to build up peasant resistance to Batista without starting a premature American intervention; Mao's party survived the massacres of the twenties, the Long March, the encirclement of Yenan, because it captured the peasant imagination with a program fitted to their wants and culture. Had Lenin, Fidel, or Mao been members of the groups they inspired in Brazil, they would have either wasted their lives waiting for the objective revolutionary conditions to appear—or they would have been killed.

Only Mao Tse-tung and Ho Chi-minh, among the great revolutionaries of our times, were peasants. Their nationalism and pragmatism sprang from the wisdom of countless generations who tilled the land of the nations they built. The story of their success is a lesson in political flexibility, as well as daring and sacrifice. Having never doubted the correctness of their strategic goals, they accepted all the tactical alliances that might further them and refused to yield to any pressures, domestic or foreign, which they felt were detrimental to their people's struggles. Mao's writings teach above all that revolution must soak itself in the people's reality in order to advance and conquer. Their beauty and universal message lies in their intrinsically Chinese character. It is, then, somewhat absurd for Maoists to brandish the Little Red Book as if it held the formula for global revolution, a blueprint to be applied everywhere. One can hardly imagine anything farther from Mao's thought than trying to organize a peasant's war in the industrialized societies of France or Germany. Even in Brazil, where conditions sometimes seem similar to those he analyzed in China, an uncritical transposition can only lead to disaster.

Most forces committed to the transformation of Brazil's social structures feel the need for a revolutionary theory deeply rooted in our reality. The lack of such a theory lies at the bottom of lost decades of struggle.

The Communist Party failed to provide this theory. Its evolution shows a peculiar adaptation to Soviet foreign policy goals, a circumstance that made the CP develop unevenly and lose many opportunities.

In 1935 when the U.S.S.R. was an outcast surrounded by a capitalist world, with hardly any say in the preservation of peace or the organization of international life, Brazil's CP attempted a military putsch unrelated to the Party's actual strength. Influenced by the then militaristic outlook of its secretary general, Luiz Carlos Prestes (who in 1924 had commanded a 3,000-man column through 7,000 miles of ceaseless combat in one of history's longest marches) the CP tried a shortcut to revolution. The uprisings in Rio de Janeiro and Recife gave Getúlio Vargas a pretext for consolidating his dictatorship. It was a foolish adventure, paid for with ten years of murderous repression. Prestes himself was arrested and kept under conditions so terrible that his lawyer could best defend him by invoking the law for the prevention of cruelty to animals.

In the thirties, a time of triumphant reaction all over the world, the Brazilian Communist Party seemed to be the only effective opposition to fascism. Working underground, it grew and accumulated strength. Students and intellectuals were attracted by anti-fascist ideals. Workers joined because the Party defended their economic interests and offered them a chance to share in its internal decision-making process. There was very little success, however, in politicizing peasants. After some unprofitable efforts, the Party centered its action in the cities.

When, in 1945, Prestes was released from prison in the wake of the Allies' victory, the Soviet Union's situation in the world had been radically altered, and Brazil's CP line was changed. The new super-power had its hands full with establishing buffer states against future aggressions of the capitalist nations, especially Germany. It could not afford to extend its lines to areas not vital for its survival. The decolonization process which got underway in Asia and Africa did not change American spheres of influence in Latin America. On the contrary, U.S. domination was reinforced and its nuclear monopoly made a challenge impossible. Therefore, Prestes led the Party in search of a national bourgeois revolution. The idea was that if the country modernized its capitalistic structures, not only would emerging Brazilian economic interests clash with America's imperialistic ones, but internal contradictions would become so acute that the ground soil for social revolution would be more easily laid. This plan prescribed non-violent methods and tactical alliance with progressive bourgeois sectors. It was adhered to even after anti-Party persecutions started again, and after the Cold War entered its belligerent phase in 1948. With slight alterations it survived through the fifties, reinforced by the de-Stalinization process brought about by Khrushchev's report to the CP Congress. During the early sixties the CP became a political mongrel, when opportunism and the rush to sinecures offered by Goulart deeply corrupted the Party's structure.[6]

During the long months immediately following the 1964 coup the Party devoted most of its energies to rebuilding the underground network necessary to the survival of its leadership and organization. When internal discussions finally began, self-criticism was centered not on the Party's conciliatory attitude during Goulart's regime, but on its supposedly inflexible attitude towards conciliation. "We were carrying on the struggle against an appeaser government, our main objective being to unmask it before the masses. . . . Instead

[6] The bibliography on Brazil's Communist Party is quite extensive. The reader who is interested should look up Astrojildo Pereira (the Party's secretary general from 1922–29), *Formação do PCB 1922–28*, Rio de Janeiro, Editorial Vitoria, 1962, and Leoncio Basbaum, *Historia Sincera da República*, São Paulo, Edições LB, 1962, vol. II and III. For the evolution of the Party line from the disastrous 1935 putsch to its short-lived legal period, the basic document is a collection of Luiz Carlos Prestes' speeches *Problemas Atuais da Democracia*, Rio de Janeiro, 1945. A rather confused but bibliographically rich attempt to establish the intellectual influences on Brazil's CP is Vamireh Chacon, *História das Idéias Socialistas do Brasil*, Rio de Janeiro, Editora Civilação Brasileira, 1965, pp. 321–48. Some works published in English are Robert Alexander, *Communism in Latin America*, New Brunswick, New Jersey, 1957, chapter VII; "Brazil's CP: A Case Study in Latin American Communism," in *Problems of Communism*, No. 5, September–October 1955, pp. 17–26; Rollie A. Poppino, *International Communism in Latin America*, Glencoe, 1964, pp. 70–77 and 143–44. Some documents can be found in Luis Aguiller's *Marxism in Latin America*, New York, Alfred A. Knopf, 1968, pp. 139–44, 161–64, 250–56. An excellent study of the early years of Brazil's CP is found in the unpublished doctoral dissertation of Paulo Sergio Pinheiro at the Fondation Nationale de Sciences Politiques, "La Fin de la Première République au Brésil," Paris, 1971.

of concentrating our fire on American imperialism and its domestic agents, we directed our attacks mainly against the policy of conciliation, with the result that imperialism received only the secondary or side effects of these attacks. A false evaluation of reality prevented us from seeing that the correlation of social forces during the last months of Goulart's government was daily becoming less and less favorable to the national-democratic forces." The conclusion reached at this point was that "the root of our errors lies in a petty bourgeois misconception of the Brazilian revolution. It is a conception that sees revolution not as a mass phenomenon but rather as the result of group action and, at best, of action by the Party."[7]

Inspired by Lenin's analysis of the Bolsheviks' survival after the defeat of the 1905 revolution and by the concept of strategic retreat, the Party expelled its São Paulo leadership—Carlos Marighela, Joaquim Câmara Ferreira, and others —who were influenced by the Cuban experience and were calling for an immediate armed reaction against the dictatorship. A "rightist" faction that rose against arbitrary centralism and personality cult, was also expelled because "when we discard repressive control we generally also give up the systematic use of any control, including control in its most elementary expression—that of tasks to be accomplished," said Prestes in self-justification in 1970.

The result of this "strategic retreat" policy was several splits and the loss of most of the CP's middle-class bases. Marighela's Ação Libertadora Nacional (ALN) as well as the originally Trotskyist groups Política Operaria (POLOP), Vanguarda Armada Revolucionaria Palmares (VAR) and the formerly nationalist Vanguarda Popular Revolucionaria (VPR) presented a concrete alternative in the form of urban guerrillas which were to operate at once, while the countryside would be approached by a mobile military column that would serve as the starting point for a widespread peasant uprising. On the other hand, classic political work through

[7] These quotations come from the CPB's self-critical document published by *Principios*, No. 108, Santiago de Chile, August, 1965, pp. 142–62. The English translation I used is found in Luiz Aguillar, op. cit., pp. 250–56.

trade unions was severely hampered by police repression. Modern identification techniques and new American equipment made it almost impossible to shift known militants from state to state, from one trade union to another. The government's permanent repression against hostile labor leaders deprived the unions of whatever usefulness they might have had in promoting class struggle. When strikes became crimes against national security and labor leaders were obliged to produce a police-issued ideological certificate, the Party lost its normal communication channels with unorganized working masses. Thus, not only did its presence on the political scene dwindle, but its theoretical production came almost to a halt. Cornered by repression, forced into defensive ideological positions by leftist groups that denounced its immobility, it published a series of tactical diagnoses and promoted several short-term alliances with bourgeois forces, but it was unable to formulate a general program with strategic goals.

Urban guerrilla groups eroded much of the Communist Party's strength, especially in Rio de Janeiro and São Paulo. Carlos Marighela's attempt to weld together traditional forms of mass politics and armed struggle galvanized young militants. His ideas, as summarized by Conrad Detrez, a Belgian ex-member of ALN and his last interviewer, were: "Thesis—priority to political over military work, exaltation of the proletariat's role, a strategy of alliances with the so-called 'nationalist' or 'progressive' bourgeois forces under the leadership of the orthodox CPs (up to 1960). Antithesis—priority to military over political work; the discovery of the peasantry whose wretched standards of living should prompt them to join the struggle (spontaneism) a strategy based on the guerrilla *foco*[8] as developed by Fidel Castro and Che Guevara and systemized by Régis Debray (up to 1967). Synthesis—the union from the very beginning of military and political work, the simultaneous interplay between the guerrilla van-

[8] The *foco* theory holds that when objective conditions for revolution are ripe a group of guerrillas can trigger it by starting to fight from a well-chosen point (*foco*). The guerrillas should have absolute freedom to decide both the political and the military aspects of the struggle.

guard and mass movements and the tactical liaison between the urban proletariat and the peasantry with the aim of starting a revolutionary war. Organizing itself in this perspective ALN tried to surpass Castroism without denying it, therefore avoiding the deadlock of Castro-Guevarism. Rather than unconditionally adopting Maoism, Carlos Marighela proposes to combine work with the masses of a classic Communist type—which should not be disregarded—with both urban and rural forms of armed struggle."[9]

Marighela was expelled from the Communist Party in December 1966, after his thesis was turned down by the Party's Congress. In 1967 he started to act with a few followers who became members of the ALN, but it took some time both for the police and the revolutionary sympathizers to realize that the mysteriously well-planned holdups represented the beginning of the urban guerrilla. After 1968, when this became known, ALN grew rapidly. Its alliance policies were broad enough to include radicalized non-Marxist, mostly Catholic, and unaligned members of the middle classes. Its aggressive political outlook, which ended a stagnant phase of discussions, had the appeal of simplicity. "A united front is firepower, a united front is revolutionary action and nothing else," wrote Marighela, "and though the main enemy of our people is American imperialism, our country cannot be freed if at the same time the great capitalists and landowners are not expelled from power and replaced by a popular revolutionary government."[10]

The use of only one weapon, the urban guerrilla, against a complex and powerful enemy was to cost Brazil's revolution many defeats and claim Marighela's life but, at the time, it was a sweet siren song for a raped generation and Marighela defended himself against accusations of "militarism" and of following too closely some of the elitist revolutionary concepts of Régis Debray's foco theory. In practice, however, he subscribed to Debray's thesis, which said that in Brazil, as in other Latin American countries, the political conditions

[9] Conrad Detrez, in *Carlos Marighela, Pour la Libération du Brasil*, Paris, Editions du Seuil, 1970, p. 41.

[10] Carlos Marighela, *Ratificación de una Tesis*, La Habana, Tricontental, January 1970, p. 71–76.

for revolution already exist and that all that is needed to spread it through the masses is the spark of military action. Debray wrote that "in Vietnam the military pyramid of the liberation forces is built from the apex down—the permanent forces first, the foco, then the semi-regular forces in the vicinity of the foco and, lastly or after victory, the militia."[11]

Instant revolution is always attractive to young people, impatient as they are of the slow-moving organizing in the classic Leninist tradition. Marighela, while rejecting the idea of forming a foco in a sparsely populated area, where it would draw the enemy's concentrated fire, was never able to implement or even to explain in detail the alternative tactic of a mobile military column. What he did organize was a comb-like structure of interconnecting urban focos. These small armed groups had no intention of overthrowing the government or of attempting to gain nationwide power. Their role recalled what Debray called the armed propaganda effect of rural guerrillas. The daring blows of these groups were to prove that resistance was possible. This would make it easier to recruit new militants, would broaden the guerrillas' social base, help to implant hostile forces in the cities, next to the country's decision-making complex and to provide rear-guard support for a liberation army's activities in the countryside.

The most successful armed propaganda exploits in Brazil were the kidnaping of foreign diplomats, ransomed against political prisoners. The first to be taken, U. S. Ambassador Charles Elbrick, kidnaped by an ALN-MR-8 commando on September 4, 1969, set the trading rules that were to prevail for some time.

Elbrick was kidnaped at a perfect time for the revolutionaries. A military junta had just replaced ailing President Costa e Silva and the Americans had not yet developed their non-negotiating policy, adopted when their diplomats started to be picked up like ripe apples by every guerrilla group on the American continent.

The first ambassadorial kidnaping in Brazil's history of urban guerrilla activities might have ended in the death of the kidnapers had the hostage not been the representative of

[11] Régis Debray, *Revolution in the Revolution*, New York, Monthly Review Press, 1967.

the U.S., a man whose status in Brazil is only slightly below that of a British Viceroy of India in Victorian days. The State Department put pressure on the Brazilian junta to save its ambassador's life. The junta, after painful discussions decided to accept the revolutionaries' conditions. It published their manifesto and kept a firm grip on a group of hard-line officers who wanted to shoot a ransomed prisoner every half-hour in a public square until the ambassador was released. At the last moment, when the prisoners were waiting at Rio's airport to board the plane that would take them to Mexico, the field was occupied by a hard-line paratroop company bent on preventing their departure. The government finally made the paratroopers obey orders and the plane left for Mexico.

Once the Brazilian government had accepted one bargain, the diplomatic precedent was set. The junta's successor couldn't very well reverse the precedent by refusing to deal with the kidnapers of the Japanese consul-general in São Paulo, the German or the Swiss ambassadors. However, the negotiations that dragged on for more than a month preceding the Swiss ambassador's release in January 1971, during which the government refused to exchange the most important guerrilla leaders, apparently blunted this revolutionary weapon. Since the enemy was allowed to choose whom he wanted to free, kidnaping became politically unprofitable.

A tactic employed too often allows the enemy time to work out countertactics. The U.S. government's countertactic is now to refuse to deal with kidnapers and to advise governments in its sphere of influence to do likewise. But even if this policy had not been adopted, Brazil's revolutionary movements probably would have revised its tactics. There was a change in public opinion. The kidnaping of the American ambassador had been extremely popular. It humiliated the imperialist superpower and its local puppets. The happy ending made a perfect scenario—the bad guys were left flat on their faces and no blood was spilled. But the public saw little connection between the Japanese, German, and Swiss diplomats and the hated dictatorship. Counterpropaganda, skillfully playing on popular sentimentalism and the dangers suffered by seemingly neutral hostages, began to sap the revolutionaries' position. As a whole the political balance of kidnapings probably tips in favor of the dictatorship, because the advantage of freeing a few militants would be annulled by public disapproval and subsequent increased repression. One of the golden rules of revolutionary struggle is not to engage in political activities which are too far from the masses' understanding, since no revolution can prosper without their support.

To kidnap an ambassador is not extremely complicated. It is much easier, for instance, than organizing a massive jailbreak (such as the Tupamaros orchestrated in Montevideo in August 1971), or attack a military barracks. All that is needed for a kidnaping is a careful study of the ambassador's habits and schedules, a few stolen cars, a small, determined group of fighters, and a safe place to keep the hostage. Almost any urban guerrilla organization can provide this.

Charles Elbrick's kidnaping is a good example of how an almost amateurish group can pull off a spectacular job. The idea occurred to a student group called MR-8, Movimento Revolucionario 8, formed by dissident members of Rio's Communist Party Youth. One of the girls flirted with an embassy guard and noted down the ambassador's very regular hours, his car route and the weakness of his escort. Another girl rented a house and paid for it with a check signed by one of the group's members, a mistake that led to the kidnapers almost immediately. When plans were ready the group contacted Carlos Marighela, who sent three of his aides to provide a somewhat more professional cover in case a shootout proved necessary. It wasn't. The ambassador was smoothly whisked away, but a few hours later, on a neighbor's tip, the hideout was discovered and surrounded. Only the junta's strict orders to save the ambassador's life prevented the house from being stormed.

For the revolutionaries one of the most dangerous phases of a kidnaping is the hostage's release. If the police know where the hostage is, they will try to corner the kidnapers right after the prisoner is released. In Elbrick's case this was avoided because the revolutionaries threatened a pursuing car with a machine gun. One of them, however, was so green that he went to his family's house for some clothes and was caught.

German Ambassador Von Hollenben's kidnaping on June 11, 1970, was not as easy as Elbrick's. Extremely well planned, it involved fifteen people and five cars. In contrast to Elbrick, who had left his bodyguards at home, Von Hollenben was accompanied by four policemen, one of whom was killed. The ambassador's hiding place was discovered only several months later when the police arrested and tortured one of the revolutionaries who had guarded him. The same operational skill was displayed for the kidnapings of the Japanese consul-general and the Swiss ambassador.

The first phase of Brazil's urban guerrillas began to close on November 4, 1969. Carlos Marighela was on the verge of unifying the several groups then in operation. He was murdered before he could get a sufficiently strong collective leadership going or root his organization deep enough. The disappearance of such an experienced, renowned and able leader; the arrest of his closest lieutenants; and, on October 24, 1970, the death of Joaquim Câmara Ferreira, ALN's best organizer and Marighela's successor, delayed the ideological debate among revolutionary organizations. The lack of a clear political strategy and the absence of one dominant group has since prevented the formation of a truly united front.

"While I live, I don't see how I live." The words of the peasant woman taking stock of her situation could be applied to some revolutionary movements. The permanent activism of urban guerrillas, the fearful repression they face, the complex nature of Brazil's society, etc., all hinder the development of a revolutionary theory able to mobilize massive popular support. Having numerous immediate problems to cope with—of which survival is not the least—the theoretical output by these groups is somewhat skimpy.

"Without revolutionary theory there is no revolutionary praxis." From 1964 to 1967 the military took advantage of the Left's disarray to force their plans down the throats of the Brazilian masses. At that moment Ação Popular's message of radical commitment outside the frame of Marxist-Leninist parties promised to be sufficiently broad to provide people from different social and political environments with a bridge to revolutionary activity. Its option appeared to be firm but flexible enough to accommodate a wide range of freedom fighters, as does Vietnam's National Liberation Front. The promise disappeared in the fog of radical verbalization. The way to allow plurality of political options within a single revolutionary movement—a pre-condition for revolutionary success in Brazil—has yet to be found.

Brazilian revolutionaries, who so often try to import models and ideas from other peoples' struggles, should ponder Cuba's most original lesson. As Leo Huberman and Paul Sweezy put it: "The most important fact about the Cuban revolution is that it was the first time—ever, anywhere—that a genuine socialist revolution has been made by non-Communists."[12] Fidel Castro acknowledges the unorthodox nature of the revolution he led. Speaking to K. S. Karol about the tiny percentage of real revolutionaries among Cuba's population on the eve of Batista's overthrow, he states, "None of this fits in with the scheme of Karl Marx. But we transgressed against the laws of History by making our revolution in the first place. I suppose we shouldn't have made it."[13] In point of fact the laws of history are less rigid and harder to interpret than many doctrinaire revolutionaries would like them to be. Victorious revolutions teach—in Cuba as in China or Vietnam—that only those with sufficiently adaptable tactics tread to the end the long road to power.

The possibility of making AP the starting point of a broad revolutionary front was destroyed by the sudden sectarianism of its leadership—and by its changes of mind. Right after the military coup some of the movement's top members took a *foquist* position: they helped plan guerrilla bases in the forests near Rio, São Paulo and Belo Horizonte. When one of these bases fell without a shot and the others collapsed by themselves, they grew disenchanted with what they labeled "the Cuban model." Their search for new ideas led to the discovery of Mao Tse-tung. They found in him the global explanation of the process of revolutionary creation in an underdeveloped country. His totalizing approach was well fitted to the group's urge for intellectual security and for

[12] Leo Huberman and Paul Sweezy, *Cuba, Anatomy of a Revolution*, New York, Monthly Review Press, 1960, p. 154.

[13] K. S. Karol, *Guerrillas in Power*, New York, Hill and Wang, 1970, p. 479.

a universe shut to all doubts born from previous Catholic convictions. They adopted the new creed with the uncritical fervor of converts. And they turned against their old sources with the zeal of those who want to wipe from their minds the memories of past errors. They soon were rabidly opposed to anything that might have a religious inspiration. Those who kept their Christian beliefs were expelled and though AP members still tried to use the Church's material possibilities they unequivocally broke away from it.

For a long time AP's leadership and militants continued to be recruited from the middle classes, but definite resolutions were adopted to change radically the movement's social composition. The decision, politically justified and perhaps even necessary, was carried to extreme limits. Any member who would not become an unskilled worker or peasant was branded a rightist deviationist and expelled. No alternate tasks were offered to those unwilling to quit their social background. AP was thus quickly reduced to a small core of dedicated missionaries—heroic, no doubt—but whose political impact on national politics will only be felt, if at all, in the very long run.

A moment of sectarianism can destroy years of work. Recently AP revised some positions, chose broader policies and opened itself to contacts with other revolutionaries. But the bridges it had started to build were destroyed. Militants had become discouraged or had joined other organizations or pursued individual tasks in the midst of ideological confusion. And, perhaps most important, the dialogue with the Catholic Church had been wasted.

The task of forming a united revolutionary front still goes unfulfilled. Each day that passes with Brazil's left still divided is a day the dictatorship uses to perfect its repression.

CHAPTER IX

CHRISTIANS AND REVOLUTION

Whoever is exposed to a formal Catholic education will later have to overwork the Holy Spirit to become a Christian. Christianity is presented there as nothing but a mediocre set of rules. The brainwashing, dehumanizing teachings inflicted upon defenseless children and adolescents hide Christ's true message.

The Catholic Church landed in Latin America on horseback and was spread by the sword. We were baptized in blood. The Church never shed its alliance with the conquerors and historical tradition only enhanced its Constantinian deformations. Throughout the centuries it defended a society based on oppression and taught the people to accept injustice. It amassed wealth based on the hunger of others. It shared the privileges of the dominant classes whose children it trained and fed. It blessed the exploiters and deceived the exploited. It faced the centuries unchanged, guilty of murder and plunder. The formal separation between Church and state brought about by the twentieth century enabled cardinals and bishops to disclaim responsibility for the crimes of secular authorities in the elegant and hollow pastoral letters they issue from their palaces.

Charity, the foremost Christian virtue, was the greatest victim of the political marriage between the Catholic Church and Latin America's dominant classes. It was killed the day Spanish slave-drivers expelled from the New World Friar Bartolomé de Las Casas, advocate of human rights for the Indians, and were supported by the hierarchy's complicity. The absence of charity is further evidenced in the Church's share of Crown taxes and its financial dependence upon the Republics; and we see it today, through pompous speeches calling for law and order, condemning "subversive" violence. What the Catholic Church once called its "charitable" work was, at best, a political function delegated by the ruling classes. The hospitals, orphanages, and schools it maintained were a means of returning some income to the dispossessed, keeping social tensions under control, enhancing the Church's influence over the poor, and thus strengthening its appeals for obedience and conformity.

Whenever the "charitable" work served as a spearhead for Western "civilization" the results were even worse. In the Amazon forests, for instance, well-meaning missionaries have spread terrible human and cultural destruction. Their dedication killed more Indians than the gold-diggers' guns. Amazon Indians have no inbuilt defenses against most civilized diseases. German measles can wipe out whole tribes. Common colds can be as murderous as a medieval plague. Missionaries force Indian girls to wear shirts, which they accepted as a welcome protection against mosquitoes. The girls are used to diving into the river six to ten times a day. Normally they are given only one or two shirts which they don't bother to take off before bathing. Night chills on the Amazon are sudden and biting. The combination of wet cloth and cold air is often a first step to pneumonia and death. Other "civilized" blessings such as sugar and organized labor are no less disrupting than prudishness. Sugar rots the Indian's magnificent teeth. Individually paid labor destroys the tribes' production structures. As missionaries succeed in integrating their flock into the Christian, capitalist world, the once healthy and free savages become sick, exploited wrecks.

"Do you accept the God of the Portuguese?" This sixteenth century formula, used in India by the soldiers of the Great Albuquerque and other pious conquerors as an alternative to the sword, could well be translated in present-day Brazil as "Do you accept the God of the rich?" "Rich" and "for the rich" are the services offered by a Catholic bureaucracy whose Evangelical origins are lost in a forest of rules, conformity and fears.

A church, implanted in a given place at a given time,

becomes an original sociological institution, even if it is part of a global organization and is inspired by transcendental values. The institution develops its norms which burden and sometimes bury the values. These norms tend to gather importance and they become ends in themselves. A ritual religion begins to form, progressively deforming the spiritual message. The church becomes a utilitarian machine, dispensing social credit to birth, marriage, public and private success, and handing out insurance against the hazards of eternity at the moment of death. It gives consolation to meek, downtrodden women and teaches the oppressed to endure. As it moves away from the liberating teachings of its founder, this church truly becomes the opium of the people. Internally it adopts corporation structures and relations. A system of vertical domination is established, with the bishop-manager standing high above his priest-executives and completely disconnected from the laymen-clients. Under such circumstances the only way to reinstate the original transcendental values—charity, brotherhood, love, freedom—is to subvert the system through a cultural revolution. Only by a relentless questioning of the rules and hierarchy can a part of the Church transform the whole and turn the ritualistic society back into a Christian community.

In Brazil a group of laymen, priests, and a few bishops have been trying for several years to do just this. They were supported by the Vatican when they tried to modernize the administrative machinery. Rome had long worried about the liturgical somnolence of the Brazilian people, statistically the largest Catholic flock in the world. Research on Sunday Mass attendance and other liturgical obligations showed that religious realities and official census data are quite different matters. Most of those who declared themselves "Catholics" were Catholic only by cultural tradition and in fact were totally severed from the Church. In the larger cities only 8 to 15 per cent of the population attend Sunday Mass regularly, mostly women and children. In the countryside the Church is basically regarded as a miracle worker to be appeased and flattered. There are great annual pilgrimages to sanctuaries such as Bom Jesus da Lapa on the São Francisco River, where pilgrims seek cures for their diseases and vast processions are made to ask for rain in drought periods, but religious perception seldom goes beyond the magic quests of the primitive. Consequences of such a situation are a steep decrease in the number of candidates for the priesthood and a loosening of the Church's influence. Cardinal Giovanni Montini (Paul VI), when Secretary of State, was well aware of this and supported Dom Helder Camara's effort in 1952 to establish a co-ordinating agency for pastoral activities and a centralized decision-making body for the hierarchy through the CNBB, National Commission of Brazilian Bishops. Other modernizing drives, such as training programs for laymen, long-term planning, financial reform of Church budgets and reform of divinity studies were also approved by the Vatican. In fact, Pope John XXIII practically intervened in the Brazilian Church by sending an ultimatum calling for the updating of its activities which resulted first in an emergency pastoral plan, then in 1966 in the General Pastoral Plan adopted by CNBB.

The progressive bishops and priests were also supported by the Vatican when they shifted the emphasis of the Church's official rhetoric from moralizing to social concern. This followed the general transformations brought about by John XXIII to the universal Church. The encyclicals *Mater et Magistra* and, especially, *Pacem in Terris,* published on Easter 1963, reinforced the leverage of the progressive clerics and forced many conservative prelates to go along with their criticism of Brazil's social structures. Another factor favoring the progressive Catholic minority was the nuncio's position. Monsignor Armando Lombardi, papal nuncio to Brazil from 1954 to 1964, was aware of the country's social needs and of the Church's shortcomings. He held weekly consultations with Dom Helder Camara. Since during his tenure the Vatican created 109 new bishops and 24 archbishops in Brazil, almost doubling the Brazilian hierarchy, Monsignor Lombardi was influential in altering somewhat the political balance within the hierarchy by supporting progressive priests for many of the vacancies.

It is, unfortunately, a far cry from words to actions. An abyss lies between the will to modernize the Church's administration, to give a relevant ring to ecclesiastical rhetoric, and actually to transform entrenched habits. When the socially committed Catholics tried to break old political alliances they were advised to be cautious. When they started to organize the dispossessed, they were warned. And when persecution fell upon them, they were abandoned.

Ever since the military coup all those engaged in organizing against the prevailing social order—in the fields, the mills, or the schools—have been persecuted. Repression is the only democratic institution left in Brazil. It strikes everyone, making no distinction between motivations: for the police it doesn't matter if someone is promoting social awareness among peasants or *favelados* (slum dwellers) because of Marxist, Christian, or simply humanitarian belief. All are included within the vague and all-embracing definition of subversion and are equally punished. As a result of this repressive norm Catholics became the most conspicuous and easily identified group among Brazil's political prisoners.

As I went through Recife's jails and gathered information from political prisons all over the country, I started to stumble upon this unusual group of victims. Their presence puzzled me. It didn't fit into my prejudices or correspond to my knowledge. I had followed with a distracted eye the political evolution of the Church's writings. The accounts a few friends working with JUC, Catholic University Youth, gave me about their revolutionary option had been stored in the back of my mind as something irrelevant and bizarre. I imagined that both the committed statements and JUC's position sprang from the Church's opportunistic tendencies. Left seemed the way of the future. The hierarchy's statements generally followed governmental initiatives and both were strangely coincidental. For a neutral observer there was little to suggest that a profound shift of political attitudes was developing within the Catholic Church. It looked as if the old Church-state marriage was exploring new possibilities allowing the partners some populist escapades.

To discover that the change was genuine, that these were people willing to back their commitments with their lives, was something of a revelation. I was attracted by these strange followers of a religion so radically different from the one I had once known and rejected. I tried to understand them. Contacts, discussions, explanations developed into friendships strengthened by common interests, common tasks, and mutual trust. A priest would ask me to negotiate with an embassy the granting of political asylum to someone he was hiding. While we drove from one ambassador to another, trying to keep calm in the face of diplomatic indifference and then sharing the joy of depriving the torturers of another victim, we talked. Or a woman would appear with a text to be published and we would discuss the situation of JOC, the Workers Catholic Movement, or the bishops.

From politics our talks passed on to Church affairs and, finally, to religion. The commitment of this breed of Christians was directly inspired by the Gospels. Christ was to them a very real human being whose insertion in time changed their own lives. They discussed His teachings objectively, using their minds and faith to discern the meaning of each text and its relevance to them. They tried to demystify Christianity by retaining the original values that had been hidden by rules. Theirs was a search for the human dimension of God, the only one they thought capable of enhancing divinity. Their flexible religious procedure seemed, however, to provide them with goals more exacting and ambitious than those set by the "orthodox" Catholics I had known. And though their choice was one of permanent questioning, of endless investigation, it provided them with a sense of security not common among those who hide within a closed universe in which all doubts have already been answered by Scholastic philosophy. To be sure of one's choice is a joyful blessing. I found that these strange Christians were some of the gayest people I had ever met. They faced life with humor and optimism, enjoying both its pleasures and its challenges.

I joined these "catacomb Christians" by sharing their political activities and slowly began to get interested in their religious opinions. They guided me through readings of the Gospels. They were extremely discreet and went to great lengths so that I would not feel they were proselytizing. I hesitated, I stumbled, I was terribly afraid of not being able to follow the demands an option of this sort would set for me and I tried to cover up these fears with metaphysical doubts. All the while they amiably stood back, though always ready to discuss any subject which might have become a problem for me.

During the first years of military dictatorship in Brazil radical Christian groups were discussing two theoretical problems which had to be solved in order to give greater effectiveness to their political actions—Marxism and violence. The questions were: Can a Christian be a Marxist? Can a Christian resort to violence in order to achieve social justice? Most of the groups' members gave a positive answer on both counts. They stayed together building structures parallel to those of the Church. Those who refused Marxism and violence either drifted into political inactivity or stayed within the Church's social organizations.

The main arguments for the compatibility between a Christian and a Marxist option were developed by student and worker groups highly influenced by the overtures toward Christianity then being made by two European Communists —France's Roger Garaudy and Italy's Luigi Longo. Both considered the problem of Marx's atheism a false one. Longo held that Marx denounces only alienating religion—the sort of religion existing in his time. Garaudy argued that Marxism is an effort to end man's alienation and that this is precisely the sense of Christ's message before it was deformed by the sociological churches throughout history.

Brazil's radical Catholics argue that the Gospel does not offer an ideology to guide the social and political actions of Christians. What it does is to urge them to be the co-builders of history, a mission to be accomplished through social and political decisions. A Christian therefore must look elsewhere for an ideology, a fact the Catholic Church takes into account when it tries to formulate its "social teachings."

The "social teachings" of the Church are found in papal encyclicals of the last one hundred years. At best they are an ethical blueprint with little scientific background, written in a vague way and stuffed with contradiction. They see the world from the guilt-ridden standpoint of a dominant class in a developed society. Their criticism of both communism and capitalism offers no alternative and sounds rather too strong against the first to be really opposed to the second. But these "social teachings" do not actually bind Catholics.

If they did the Church would be a political party. It is a sociological aberration, not a model, that in some countries—especially Italy—the Catholic Church is far too close to the Christian Democratic Party. The options in Brazilian politics—perceived at the time this discussion was under way—were conservative, reformist, or revolutionary. A conservative option would support the military dictatorship and its plans for a dependent and socially stratified system that would forever deny equal opportunities and human living conditions to most Brazilians. A reformist regime could at best alleviate the most urgent social needs, incorporating into the system some sectors of the population, but could not free the country from North American dominance and distribute a wealth that, produced by all, should be shared by all. To side with reform in the end would mean to reinforce the existing class system and its injustices. A revolutionary transformation of society was seen by many as the only honest alternative. Marxist analysis was the only scientific instrument available to guide those who wanted to achieve this transformation, for not only does it provide an intellectual tool able to analyze change on a global scale but it also draws a sociopolitical model in which justice can be preserved better than in the liberal-capitalistic ones of the Western developed world.

The discussion of models is always a disappointing one because the historical situations that conditioned the development of one country can never be reproduced in another. It is, however, a trap into which everyone falls, since it is easier to argue from concrete examples than from abstractions. The models capitalism produced after ravaging and plundering the world for centuries influenced the discussion's results. The most successful capitalist country, the United States, achieved immense wealth and power, but it seems unable to extend material well-being to a sizable part of its population, to absorb its ghettos and heal its social problems. If the best capitalism can produce is a sick society, torn by prejudices, at war with its youth and willing to commit the most atrocious crimes in order to preserve its domination over other peoples, why try to reproduce it? It is true that paradise on this earth is yet to be found, but if some day it materializes, private ownership of the means of production will certainly not be the base of its society.

The discussion about violence and non-violence flowed from the decision to work for socialism. Once again the groups thought that the Church's recent condemnations of revolutionary violence are not only unsound but hypocritical. Invoked today to disapprove of socialism, traditional theology actually justifies violence in no uncertain terms. Thomas Aquinas listed the conditions that free tyrannicides from sin; crusades were not only tolerated but financed and glorified; and texts about "just wars" abound. Doctrine evolved in a good way when it started to reject wars, but then why not condemn with equal vigor all acts of aggression, every kind of violence? How can the Vatican's resounding declarations against revolutionary struggles bind Catholics when its silence over the massacres of Jews in Nazi Europe and American atrocities in Vietnam still rings so loudly in their memories? Why should priestly service to Christ be better personified by Francis Cardinal Spellman, garbed in combat fatigues blessing an invading army in Indochina, than by Father Camilo Torres, who chose to free his people by grasping a gun, and who paid for his dream with his life? And if non-violence is such a Catholic virtue, where are the Catholic Martin Luther Kings, where are the Catholic Gandhis? In what continent, in what country have cardinals and bishops led marches, strikes, boycotts and sit-ins against racism, imperialism, colonialism, exploitation, all the evils they so eloquently denounce when they issue statements from their palaces? There are many Catholics who are willing to back with their lives and their freedom the causes their fidelity to Christ dictates. These are laymen, priests, nuns, even some members of the hierarchy, but they almost always taste the bitterness of solitude. When they act they find themselves isolated in their Church, estranged from its leadership, sometimes denounced by it. Helder Camara, António Fragoso and the few other bishops brave enough to speak out against the dictatorship's policy of torture and exploitation are unsupported by their colleagues and ignored by Rome. Daniel and Philip Berrigan have no cellmates clothed in purple.

The refusal to condemn the conquering violence of the

powerful and the unwillingness to support those who rise up against the colonizers is complemented by the refusal to denounce less visible injustices—"white violence" as it is called in contrast to violence that is bloody. There are, of course, sporadic texts dealing with murders committed by the simple functioning of inhuman structures—the declaration of Medellin, for instance, signed by Latin America's bishops—but they are not tuned to the Church's main preoccupations and doctrinal efforts.

The scandal represented by the Vatican's unwillingness to act against injustices can be fully realized only when one imagines the impact an organized Church with 600,000,000 could have on world affairs if it passed from words to action. We in Brazil are perhaps in a better position than most to imagine such an impact because even with its conservative majority, that disavows its more militant members, the Catholic Church has been the only force capable of restraining repression and is the only legal national institution in the country not entirely controlled by the military.

The decision of Christian revolutionary groups not to exclude from their strategy the possible use of force was not taken on theological grounds. Religious reasoning was important only to brush aside the Vatican's condemnations of violence, these being considered an obstacle to the achievement of a just society. The decisive argument was political and based on an analysis of Brazil's situation.

No one chooses violence for its own sake. Human nature, under normal circumstances, abhors it. He who wounds or kills his brother does almost as much violence to himself as to his victim. The problem lies in choosing a solution that will lead quickest to the elimination of tensions that generate violence. Cynically this could be translated as a justification for any expedient way to gain power. But if you are sure of your just use of power, there is no place for cynicism in your commitment. There is, seemingly, no difference in opening a belly with a scalpel or with a dagger: both acts are physically the same. Yet one saves, the other kills. In a political contest the choice of tactics is dictated by efficiency and the social realities that will influence the struggle's outcome.

Non-violence, though it may represent a slower way to power, can sometimes be preferable to violence. A reasonable chance of success is one precondition needed to justify the method. Also, there *must* be a possibility of dialogue out of which oppressed and oppressors can start a negotiation. In other words, those who command force must respect their enemies' lives and refrain from shooting the demonstrators. If they use their guns to murder their opponents there will shortly be no one left to be non-violent. Malcolm X used to say he was non-violent to those who were non-violent to him. In a subtle way he was expressing a radical rejection of the method, because those who hold power are always inclined to use force to protect it. But he also pointed out a political truth often forgotten by those for whom methods count more than goals—to be employed effectively, methods must be based on knowing where you stand.

Other conditions for the success of non-violent struggles are a free press and a liberal judicial system. If the protest against a local injustice cannot reach the people through mass-media exposure it will fail to acquire the symbolic meaning necessary to mobilize the oppressed. If there are no legal safeguards for human rights, those who use free speech and free assemblies against a regime will simply be put away for indefinite periods and the movement will lose its impetus.

None of these necessary conditions is present in Brazil. The press is censored, human rights suspended and the courts controlled by the Army. The government has proved repeatedly its readiness to shoot demonstrators. Marches, sit-ins and strikes would be cut down by machine guns. This is why a non-violent movement for justice and peace, even though launched by a man as popular as Dom Helder Camara, has not progressed. Our only non-violent experiment that can claim relative success is the struggle led by a group of Christian lawyers of the National Workers Front (FNT) against some crooked industrialists in São Paulo.

A radical Catholic once presented the problem of methods through this paradox: "As a Christian I know that I may not be an accomplice of the violence of capitalistic structures, but if I refuse to be an accomplice I must fight capitalism—and to do so effectively I must use violence."

The decision not to avoid violence in fighting for a socialist regime split the Catholics into different groups. Those who chose a revolutionary alternative either began helping urban guerrilla movements, generally providing the "logistical" support they needed—hideouts, transport, forged documents, etc.—or followed AP in trying to organize peasants and workers by taking on their ways and living among them. Those who preferred less radical positions followed Helder Camara's moral pressure groups, or joined the Frente Nacional do Trabalho, Church institutions related to trade unions or organizations such as MEB. One group decided that times were too rough for teamwork, always open to repression, and limited their contribution to "conscientization" tasks, individually performed and usually in a teaching context.

Moral pressure groups perform a tribunitial role. They speak for the people. Through the Church's communication system they protest at a time when all other information channels are gagged by censorship. They are the voices of the voiceless, an all-important function in a country choked by official propaganda.

Church institutions such as the Catholic Action Groups, rural trade unions and MEB (when it existed), perform the role of catalyzers of consciences. They awaken their members to Brazil's social realities, which is often frustrating because they don't offer opportunities for organized action. After a while people who are "conscientized" either become baffled and disperse, or they find on their own the political organization to which they can pledge their loyalty. Defenders of this tactic argue that the low level of political awareness among Brazilian masses indicates the necessity for a top-priority educational effort. Only after sufficiently large numbers become convinced of the need to struggle can a serious revolutionary movement develop.

Solutions for political problems entail an endless search, and discussions take a long time to unwind. Taking part in those conducted by the Catholic Left, first as an observer, then as a committed member, was excellent training for me. The exercise of collectively turning a problem inside out makes one realize how little we are taught to think and how right Bernard Shaw was when he said that most people never think during their lifetime and that he had achieved international fame by thinking three times a week. Through the meetings I attended I met many admirable men and women who, whatever course they subsequently followed, had a true love for their fellow man.

Dázinho, a pick-and-shovel miner at the bottom of the world's deepest gold mine for thirty years, was one of these. A labor leader, he had been elected to the state assembly of Minas Geraes in 1962, on a Christian Democrat ticket. He sensed, in the eight hundred dollars a congressman earned a month, an establishment trick to buy him off and weaken his connections with his fellow workers. He refused to keep more than he would have made working extra hours at the mine and gave the rest away to strike funds and needy workers. He kept his company house in Nova Lima, twenty miles from Belo Horizonte, and insisted on taking a morning tour at the pit, devoting afternoons and nights to formal politics. In 1964, when the state assembly unanimously voted to annul his parliamentary representation as well as those of the two other worker members, he needed little effort to readapt. When, months later, a military court jailed him for two years and four months, his wife and nine children were able to survive on donations scraped together by the town's miners.

Dázinho's work as a congressman had been to help organize and attend most workers' demonstrations and strikes that took place in Minas Geraes. His presence and immunity restrained the police and reassured the workers. He lost no time presenting bills or dealing with his colleagues' intrigues —"the old foxes who preyed on the poor people's blood," as he called them. He saw through the system's tricks and refused to play its games.

The group of rebellious congressmen I was later to join followed, at national level, the same kind of tactics, though none of us could match Dázinho's example. Our revolutionary commitments sprang from rational analysis, while Dázinho and other working class militants felt them as a normal consequence of their lives. Middle-class revolutionaries often feel they are taking part in an altruistic struggle which will profit others, while peasants and workers know they are fighting for themselves. They have a lasting revolutionary commitment. Revolution is their only hope and they know they can never look back on it as a "youthful error" or a folly complacently remembered when one is readmitted to the establishment. For them there is no way out: even exile, a hard but viable escape for students and professionals, is next to impossible for peasants and workers.

When Dázinho left prison some middle-class friends offered to raise the money to get him to Uruguay or Chile. He refused. "The only thing I know how to do in life," he explained, "is to dig ore out of a mine. Here I can go on living and raising a family digging ore. If I'm arrested again or if I die, my brothers will take care of my wife and children. But if I go to some foreign country where I don't know anyone and whose language I can't speak, I'm not sure to find ore to dig or brothers on whom to rely. A miner has to stay a miner and dig the mountain he knows."

Catholic working-class militants such as Dázinho are an exception in Brazil. Our working classes are formed by ex-peasants, their children, or by first- and second-generation immigrants. Migrating to the cities a peasant is uprooted from his religious environment. He no longer depends on rain or sunshine for the harvests and loses interest in the miracle-working function of Catholic pageantry. His utilitarian religiosity finds no reason for Church intervention in favor of his urban needs. On the other hand, the Church does little to attract him because its presence is weak in the shanty-towns and poor suburbs to which peasants arrive. When his new activities bring him into contact with Catholic organizations, the migrator generally finds them irrelevant if not outright hostile to his interests. The Círculos Operarios (Workers' Circles), oldest and largest of the Catholic working-class organizations, are fiercely moralizing groups with an anti-Communist obsession which has often made of them a tool against their fellow workers. Their views on class harmony, imported from Italy, are perfect for strike-busting, trade-union manipulation and other capitalist ploys. The JOC and the ACO, Catholic Action groups, which are animated by a working-class conception of social injustice, are too small

and intellectualized to provide an organizational framework
for the secularized masses.

One wonders why so many revolutionaries have remained
in the Catholic Church and why those outside—especially
orthodox Marxists—regard it as so important in Brazil. After
all, it is badly implanted among workers, wields a mostly
magic power among peasants, and disowns its middle-class
militants engaged in social struggles. This apparent contradiction can be solved only if the problem is split in two.
First, one should bear in mind that Catholic revolutionaries
see their social preoccupations as indivisible from the institution itself. To them the Church is going through a period
comparable to the Renaissance days of the Borgia Pope, Alexander VI. The difference is in the nature of the Church's
main collective sin. In Borgia's time it was primarily sin against
chastity. The sin today is against charity and the Church
barters its omission for diplomatic and administrative privileges negotiated with gangster governments.

Catholic revolutionaries long for a return to the primitive communism of early Christian times. To them redemp-
tion for the Church lies in siding unequivocally with the
oppressed and expressing this in clear political terms. Maybe
this yearning for simpler models and purer options is, in our
days of mass societies in a global village, as utopian as Jean
Jacques Rousseau's defense of a return to nature and the
idealized communities of noble savages. However earnest the
Catholics' preoccupations with their Church's internal affairs may be, their concern is based also on its great political
importance, recognized by both Catholics and non-Catholics.
This recognition leads to the second half of the problem,
the weighing of possibilities.

The Church has an enormous independent information
network. It owns dozens of radio stations, hundreds of papers,
magazines, bulletins, publishing houses, bookstores. It has a
weekly captive audience of at least ten million people. It
owns thousands of buildings—parishes, palaces, skyscrapers,
hospitals, schools, convents, missions, orphanages—every one
of which can serve as a hideout or meeting place. It commands the allegiance of 14,000 trained and disciplined
men and 40,000 obedient women who work full-time for

survival salaries. But most of all, it carries great moral weight with the urban middle classes from which the majority of its members come and is still held in reverential fear by the masses in a way unmatched by any other institution in the country. This force has always sided with the ruling classes, keeping Brazil's social structure frozen. If it dropped that allegiance, Brazil's class system could be toppled more easily.

At present the chances of changing the Church's political orientation are far-fetched but not inexistent. Brazil has some 250 bishops, one of the world's largest hierarchies. Some forty are progressive though only a handful are truly outspoken. An equal number are rigidly conservative and ready to go to any lengths to please the government—even public defense of torture. The rest are either timid, uninformed, politically aloof men or else they are professional opportunists. Unfortunately the three active cardinals lean to the right. Vicente Scherer, of Porto Alegre, is a sincere reactionary. Rio's Eugenio Sales is an authoritarian opportunist and Avelar Brandão, although sensitive and intelligent, is too much of a diplomat to commit himself to a cause. Only the archbishop of São Paulo, Evaristo Arns, not yet a cardinal, has the guts to protest when his priests are tortured or when the Death Squadron embarks on a bloody spree.[1]

[1] Though books are still rare, recent years have seen a spectacular growth in political studies on Brazil's Catholic Church. Even the Rand Corporation, the Air Force's "think-tank," produced its own paper—"Latin American Institutional Development: the Changing Catholic Church," Santa Monica, RM-6138*DOS, October 1969. Some books published in English are: Emanuel de Kadt, *Catholic Radicals in Brazil*, London, Oxford University Press, 1970; H. Lloyd Mecham, *Church and State in Latin America*, Chapel Hill, University of North Carolina Press, 1966, pp. 261–83; Thomas Sanders, *Catholic Innovation in a Changing Latin America*, Cuernavaca, CIDOC, Sondeos No. 41, 1969; Ivan Vallier, *Catholicism, Social Control and Modernization in Latin America*, Englewood Cliffs, New Jersey, Prentice Hall, 1970. Some historical works such as Ralph Della Cava's excellent *Miracle at Joaseiro*, New York, Columbia University Press, 1970, throw light on Church-state relations. Articles are more numerous. Notable are: Emanuel de Kadt, "Religion, the Church and Social Change in Brazil," in Claudio Veliz (ed.), *The Politics of Conformity in Latin America*, London, Oxford University Press, 1967; Thomas Sanders, "Catholicism and Development: the Catholic Left in Brazil," in Kalman Silvert (ed.),

The trend, however, is away from the system. One cannot teach in seminaries the social encyclicals, the harsh condemnation of the existing social order signed by Latin America's bishops at Medellin, plus sociology, history and economics and then, as though words have no relation to life, force young priests to support military dictatorships and confine their activities to rosewater sermons and intricate rituals. Many young priests keep in close touch with lay groups. They often choose to earn a living as professionals or workers, sharing the lives and ordeals of the common people. There is no better way to become politically "conscientized" in Brazil.

Speaking in general terms, the young clergy and the lay movements that were organized according to the models of French Catholic Action are pressure groups that favor social commitment and socialistic ideas. The older clergy, most female orders and some of the male ones that remain untouched by the Vatican II Ecumenical Council's theology are either reactionary or politically neutral. Lay movements that stress personal salvation, elitist attitudes, or devotions to specific saints are right-wing. Of these the largest are the Marian congregations, the fastest-growing are the Cursillos de Cris-

Churches and States: the Religious Institution and Modernization, New York, American University Field studies, 1967; and "The Church in Latin America," *Foreign Affairs*, January 1970, pp. 285–300; Norman Gall, "Latin America: Church Militant," *Commentary*, April 1970, pp. 25–37; etc. Some of the best material is not found in English. Charles Antoine, *L'Église et le Pouvoir au Brésil*, Paris, Desclée de Brouer, 1971. Helder Camara, *Revolução dentro da Paz*, Rio de Janeiro, Editora Sabia, 1968; José de Broucker, *Helder Camara, La Violence d'un Pacifique*, Paris, Fayard, 1969; António Fragoso, *Evangile et Révolution Sociale*, Paris, Le Cerf, 1969. Alain Gheerbrant, *L'Église Rebelle de L'Amérique Latine*, Paris, Le Seuil, 1969; Kosinski and Deelen, *Brasil, Igreja em Transição*, Cuernavaca, CIDOC, Sondeos No. 45; Candido Mendes, *Memento dos Vivos*, Rio de Janeiro, Editora Tempo Brasileiro, 1966. Basic material on Brazil's Church include Charles Antoine, "L'Episcopat Brésilien Face au Pouvoir," *Études*, Tome 33, July–December 1970, pp. 24–103; and Michel de Certeau, "Les Chrétiens et la Dictature Militaire au Brésil," *Politique Aujourd'hui*, No. 11, November 1969, pp. 40–53. For the persecutions suffered by Brazilian Catholics, see Marcio Moreira Alves, *O Cristo do Povo*, Rio de Janeiro, Editora Sabia, 1968, translated into Spanish and Italian.

tiandad and the most aggressive the Tradition, Family and Property, TFP.

Marian congregations are an old institution in Brazil. They were strongly promoted during the nineteenth and early twentieth centuries and their following in the interior is large, especially among women. They dodge political problems and devote their energies to processions and novenas.

Cursillos are a brainwashing technique thought up in Spain that enjoy great success among Latin American middle classes. Brought to Brazil only recently they are already a force to be reckoned with and one that will probably grow. The idea is to corral for three days a group of thirty to thirty-five men or women and bombard them for fourteen or sixteen hours a day with speeches, prayers, songs and self-vilifying testimony. Not a moment is allowed for discussions, not a second for thought, not a chance for relaxation. The organizers take clandestine snapshots of the group, watch its reactions, isolate and browbeat potential troublemakers. They use a deliberately cheap vocabulary to build up group identity. Christ is called "The Boss," who rejoices when his servants are "colorful"—that is, without sin, not the swine they were before. After seventy-two hours of this drumroll a highly emotional climate develops, leading to the cinemascopic finale. The *cursillistas* are led to a church where their families await them. Petal throwers greet them and there are warm embraces from other *cursillistas* and salvos of "Long Live The Boss." They confess their sins in public and pledge their lives to "The Boss" and His representatives on earth, the Hierarchy. *Cursillistas* are issued a small crucifix which they are urged always to carry. They should finger it for strength on momentous occasions such as a street fight with The Boss's enemies, whose numbers might include disobedient leftist Catholics. The brainwashing course is followed by weekly meetings (called *ultreyas* an old Spanish word meaning a stop on a pilgrimage road) in which the "colorful" spirit is checked up on and experiences exchanged. All this spiced, once again, with public confessions and hymns.

Private jargon, penitential breast-beating, songs, mutual support for members, the feeling of belonging to a sinless group in a sinful world, battle cries, all this goes to make a revivalist sect that stresses Catholic ritualism in its worst aspects. Strangely, some bishops considered to be progressive before 1968 encouraged the movement. Not so strangely, the conservative bishops, with their love for mindless obedience, are mad about it.

Tradition, Family and Property—TFP—is so reactionary an organization that it has been publicly upbraided several times by the Brazilian hierarchy and it enjoys the support of only a few bishops. Founded by a São Paulo professor, it is liberally financed by bankers, industrialists, and, quite possibly, the secret police, which recruits agents from among its three thousand members. TFP men (strictly a masculine affair) are monarchists and great buffs for blazons and heraldic paraphernalia. They walk the streets behind great crimson banners embroidered with golden rampant lions. Exaggeratedly devoted to the Virgin Mary, they reject the liturgical innovations and pay premium prices to have Mass said in Latin. Every afternoon they stand to attention in front of TFP's São Paulo palace, reciting a Rosary that ends with raised fist and acclamations of "Christ! Christ! Christ!"

TFP's main political activities before 1964 were denouncing Communist infiltration in Goulart's government and campaigning against agrarian reform. Its president, Plinio Correa de Oliveiro, together with bishops Geraldo Sigaud of Diamantina, and Castro Meyer of Compos, wrote a book to the effect that all social ills in the countryside would end if peasants controlled their sexual impulses better and if landowners organized proper religious services on their estates. After the military coup Communist infiltration in the Church became its main target, Dom Helder Camara and the Dominican order its "bêtes noires." Many TFP members joined the CCC, Communist Hunting Commandos, a vigilante outfit that shoots students, breaks up street demonstrations, wrecks theaters and is very likely responsible for the torture and murder on May 26, 1969, of Father Henrique Pereira Neto, a young priest in charge of Catholic student movements in Recife. More openly TFP got up a petition asking the Vatican to purge Brazil's Church from its "progressive stain." The campaign was an opportunity to harass bishops, priests, and lay movements. The articles its organizers published became so arrogant and belligerent that the Hierarchy reacted as a class and condemned them.

The self-protection instinct is the most clearly identifiable motive for the Catholic hierarchy's political moves since the military coup. The first statement published by CNBB's Central Commission after the takeover left out all the social reforming sermons the bishops had previously approved of and acclaimed the military as valiant defenders of the country against the Communist menace. At a time when the prisons were jammed with Catholic militants, when priests were forced to choose between exile and jail, when many officially Church-sponsored organizations were raided and members persecuted, the most the bishops managed to say was that accusations that Catholic Action was a Communist front were false and that the military should not view all efforts to help the dispossessed as Communist-inspired.

The same limp attitude prevailed through succeeding years. Collective episcopal documents became masterpieces of vagueness, so cautious as to be unintelligible. Some individual bishops, mainly from the northeastern poverty bowl, would not be cowed and criticized the regime and its policies. Men such as Dom Helder Camara and Dom António Fragoso, Bishop of Crateus, acquired unique stature by using their position, their credibility and their communication channels to denounce situations or acts of inhumanity. Others, like Joseph Comblin, author of a theology of revolution which is required reading for Brazilian militant Catholic groups, and the Jesuit theologian Antonio Vaz, despite the dangers, went right on thinking and publishing. Comblin was punished for his bravery and expelled from Brazil in 1972. Countless other priests and laymen went on organizing and working at grassroots level.

There were, however, a few cases in which the Hierarchy voiced its disagreement with the actions of the government. These were as a rule protests against the imprisonment of priests or judicial persecutions against bishops. Otherwise repression seems to have reinforced the clerical inclinations of many bishops: they turn their faces away when laymen are persecuted and mistreated, but protest when clergymen are the victims.

Among the hundreds of recorded torture cases in Brazil some dozen victims were ecclesiastics. The CNBB's General Conference was practically forced by the weight of evidence to touch on the subject in its 1969 declaration but, in 1971, it more promptly supported bishops who denounced torture suffered by their clergy. In the case of Dom Waldir Calheiros, bishop of Volta Redonda, who was threatened with court-martial for denouncing tortures inflicted on workers, the CNBB went as far as publishing a letter pledging its solidarity with the threatened bishop.

The political theory of most Brazilian bishops is the so-called "Polish Theory of Church-State Relations," developed by Cardinal Eugenio Sales. According to this fable the Church faces in Brazil a situation similar to the one it faces in Poland. In a country where most of the population is Catholic, the government is hostile to the Church's deepest values. A balance must be struck in order to avoid a headlong confrontation and make possible the Church's survival. In such a situation the hierarchy's first duty by definition is to survive and—therefore—to negotiate. The "Polish Theory" is, in fact, an ideological see-through blouse, a drug to calm the pangs Their Eminences may feel in their consciences (if, indeed, they have any left).

A single and simple argument suffices to show up the collaborationist character of the Church: the Brazilian military dictators go to great lengths to display their Catholic orthodoxy. They are forever courting the Church for support, approval or, at worst, neutrality. They shower money on Church institutions, make eucharistic congresses national holidays, parade in honor of the Virgin of Fatima, call for Mass to celebrate the coup's anniversary and other political events. As absolute monarchs once did, they justify their tyranny as a divine mission to defend Christian civilization. The Polish government, of course, does nothing of the sort and does not even maintain diplomatic relations with the Vatican.

Those who believe in the Church's capacity for self-reformation point out the difference between the nebulously worded and normally pro-government declarations of CNBB's annual conferences and the bolder statements published by its Central Commission. It seems the larger an assembly of bishops is, the more timid its political stand. The central commission, made up of some of the hierarchy's more dynamic and informed members has sometimes—and since 1970 quite often—stated forthright views on torture and repression. It has also avoided considering in the same light—as the general conference and Cardinal Sales have—the government's repressive violence and the violent revolutionary answers it provokes.

We are told that the bark of Peter shall not founder. If the young clergy, the committed laymen and those bishops who stand by them keep the faith, they may rally immense forces to the cause of liberation and thus make the promise hold even in Brazil.

Brazil, as most Latin American nations, is a country where revolution can be strongly influenced by Christianity, a country where Christians and Marxists can and must fight together for the same goals.

CHAPTER X

DEPENDENCE AND THE TERRORIST STATE

Dependence is a key to reality. Once you recognize it the world comes into focus. Behavior, institutions, and ideas emerge from the fog and stand out in sharp outline. Dependence is a master-servant relationship that a dominant country weaves around its satellite in many ways. In Brazil the threads of dependence are so numerous that they seem natural and you can live in their midst without noticing them. But, if the tiniest line is discerned the whole pattern suddenly becomes visible, oppressive, and unbearable. Dependence is most recognizable in economics but it is also an effort to tame the mind, teaching the people to think according to their masters' values, invading the cultural and intellectual lives of the country.

The Brazilian economy is totally dependent on foreign powers and their investments. Official figures, published to reassure Brazilians, state that only 6 per cent of our national capital is foreign-owned.[1] This already frightening percentage is misleading. The total capital of a country is formed by millions of small or barely productive properties and activities only an economist would think of adding up—stores, small farms, the houses people live in, even the tips of shoeshine boys and parking-lot keepers, pompously included among the revenues of the economy's "services" sector. This capital does not form power centers and cannot determine the econ-

[1] Delfim Neto, Brazil's Finance Minister, speaking at the Escola Superior de Guerra, ESG, in August 1971, quoted by *Veja*, September 8, 1971.

omy's control. Six per cent is an enormous amount of foreign dominance, especially if, as is the case, it is strategically placed in the most dynamic industries. Hitler's armies probably never controlled directly more than six per cent of the economies of France, Poland, and the other occupied lands. This does not mean, however, that they could not master the total economic potential of these countries in order to strengthen Germany's war effort.

The niceties of economic statistics are wasted on most Brazilians. Those of us who can understand the Finance Minister's arguments know their fallacy. We are not overjoyed when we are told that more than 90 per cent of what exists in our country is Brazilian. The fact that the state controls certain important heavy industries such as steel and oil, essential activities such as railways and road-building is not considered enough to assure our independence. We know that even in agriculture, the most Brazilianized economic sector, the market outlets, export network, international prices, packing industries and even the processing methods for instant coffee are not Brazilian. The state occupies barren, unprofitable economic space, as in the case of the railroads we bought back from the British, or that of the steel industry, which demands heavy investments for mediocre profits.

Everything we consume in our daily lives betrays a foreign presence.[2] We are bandaged at birth by Johnson & Johnson. We survive on Nestlé or Gloria Milk. We dress in synthetic clothes produced by French, British, or American firms. Our teeth are kept clean by Colgate toothpaste and Tek brushes. We wash with Lever Brothers' and Palmolive soaps, shave with Williams and Gillette. Resting in the sun we drink Coca-Cola—and now even the largest producer of cachaça, the white rum national drink, is owned by Coca-Cola. We ride Otis elevators, drive Volkswagens and Fords and ship our goods on Mercedes-Benz trucks fueled by Esso and Shell. Our rubber is Pirelli, we talk with Erics-

[2] The overwhelming foreign dominance of our consumer-goods industry inspired Paulo Martins to write a very popular satirical essay *Um Dia na Vida de Brasilino* on the line of my own description of the situation.

son telephones, communicate through Siemens telex, type on Olivetti machines and receive IBM-processed bills. We eat out of American and Canadian made cans packed by Armour, Swift, and Wilson. The Beatles' beat comes out of Phillips radios, and we dance to RCA records. Our General Electric TV sets are connected to ITT satellites. We can rely on old Bayer for aspirin, or, if trouble develops, on Squibb for antibiotics. From the comfortable Goodyear mattresses of our American hospital beds we can look through Saint-Gobain windows on gardens tended by Japanese lawnmowers. If we die (say, from lung cancer puffed from British or American cigarettes) we may finally have a chance of entering into our 94 per cent share of the economy—graveyards are owned by the Santa Casas da Misericórdia, an old Brazilian institution. But the family must pay the electricity bills to Canadian Light and Power—with money manufactured by Thomas de la Rue or by the American Bank Note Company.

Though foreign investment spreads to all industrial sectors, its most thriving area is consumer goods, produced for the groups whose income allows them to imitate the demand patterns multinational firms satisfy in their home markets. The upper and middle classes are the buyers for automobiles, refrigerators, and air conditioners, as well as office equipment and other durable and semi-durable goods that yield high profits because the state provides them with protective tariffs.

Multinational corporations migrate to foreign countries mainly to exploit the oligopolistic advantages of their markets.[3] Their fortunes are linked to the growing inequality of income distribution in the underdeveloped countries. The more the inequality concentrates income, the greater their share of the country's industries.

All-important instruments that complement foreign con-

[3] Many economists are now studying multinational corporations and their effect on world economy. Foremost among American scholars devoted to this subject are Raymond Vernon and Stephen Hymer, whose doctoral dissertation "The International Operations of National Firms: A Study of Direct Investment," Cambridge, Massachusetts Institute of Technology, 1960, unpublished, can be considered a starting point. The best Latin American analyses of the problem are those of Celso Furtado and Oswaldo Sunkel.

trol of the economy are the financial organizations that determine credit distribution and have the last word on who is going to expand and who will go bankrupt. Of the thirty investment banks existing in Brazil in 1971, ten of the top eighteen were directly controlled by foreign concerns. These banks, through which most private investment money is channeled, had an average growth rate of over 50 per cent in 1970, while the 615 largest enterprises grew 11.5 per cent and the whole economy 9 per cent. In 1971 their results were more spectacular still and many investment banks showed a better than 100 per cent profit.

American investment—at roughly 1.7 billion dollars book value—accounts for half the foreign investment in Brazil. From 1960 to 1970 it increased by 680 million dollars, of which 91 per cent was financed by reinvestment earnings. According to USAID, "during the sixties income remitted to the U.S. from Brazil exceeded the net capital outflow from the U.S. every year but three. In addition to the direct investments effects, remittances to the U.S. for sales of patents, trademarks and technical services have had an important positive effect on U.S. balance of payments averaging about 30–35 million dollars annually during the sixties."[4] In other words, Brazil exports capital to the United States. The beggar gives the millionaire a few nickels and a millionaire's fortune is made by piling up nickels.

To supervise this investment the American government has 1,400 employees in his Brazilian embassy, 54 of whom are military advisers, plus 324 Peace Corps volunteers. Senator Frank Church, commenting on these figures, said he thought they were "extremely interesting when you consider that just prior to the independence of India the British were presumably administering the country with 1,600 men and we have had something in excess of that in the past just to administer our own programs in an independent country, Brazil."

The disguised occupation under which we live is particularly distressing. The occupier's skin and language are the

[4] Statement by William A. Ellis, Director, USAID-Brazil, before the Subcommittee on Western Hemisphere Affairs, Committee on Foreign Relations, May 5, 1971, p. 215.

same as our own. He is a brother, unconscious that he performs the service for an enemy that is as much his as ours. To attack him is not as simple as attacking a foreign invader.

Empires have long valued puppet governments. Financially and politically they are cheaper than an occupying army. They are reliable and their ambitions are limited by the dominant government's interests. It is difficult for quislings to become Führers. Their power reflects only the power they are granted and it is based on foreign forces they cannot influence. They pay for it with unconditional obedience. They are unable to generate spontaneous support, a handicap that makes for a permanent need for the dominant country to step into the internal affairs of the dominated in moments of crisis, reinforcing the puppet's hand and solving factional quarrels. As each intervention leads to more blatant dominance, to greater involvement, to the unmasking of the occupation, the dominance is weakened because it becomes a source of acute dissatisfaction and nationalistic resistance. A crisis that calls for outside troops strengthens the oppressed in their will to fight the oppressor's rule.

The hazards for dominant powers mingling in their puppets' problems are apparent both on the international scene, on the one hand—an American ambassador trying to rig an election in Saigon; and on the national scene, on the other—a Brazilian dictator forced to choose a governor among feuding state oligarchies.

In Brazil foreign dominance is still politically perceived only by a minority. This allows the government lots of maneuvering space for propaganda. Industrial growth rates, mounting exports, the opening of a road through the Amazon jungle, campaigns against adult illiteracy, a football world championship—the most disparate events are manipulated as part of Project "Big Brazil," which aims to transform Brazil, under military leadership, into a superpower by the turn of the century. Statistics are thrown at the public as if they were independent entities, needing no interpretations. Governmental decisions are presented as miracles, as if the country were administered by the Wizard of Oz. Normal military attachment to secrecy plus an information void help create the impression of magic. Plans are pulled out of a top hat and

the President on duty is the chief magician of this circus.
The routine has the double advantage of endowing the government with an aura of efficiency and of curtailing discussion on matters of public interest. Only those close to the
decision-making centers, especially the National Security
Council, can discuss and influence the choice of policies. The
rest of the country is virtually powerless to alter the decisions that will determine its destiny. It is said that Hell is
the absence of God. The lack of access to technocracy and
military means total isolation from the decision-making levels of government. As industrialists and other dominant sectors of society keep the doors open to these levels by lending
the government their own technocrats, they live in paradise.
Other groups, such as the trade unions, are powerless and
are made to bear the price of their isolation.

Analyzing Napoleon III's France in *Eighteenth Bru-
maire*, Karl Marx noted the magic needs of Bonapartism.
He said Bonaparte was forced to spring constant surprises,
to carry out every day a *coup d'état* in miniature. This magic
need is also felt by Brazil's dictators.

In Brazil Bonapartism is collective rather than personal.
We are ruled by a general staff and the President is the representative of the Armed Forces. The majority of the upper
and middle classes accept the military leadership as the most
profitable to their interests. Those who refuse to goose-step
into their assigned places in society and content themselves
with pocketing the profits are terrified and forced into silence
or exile. Such general manipulation of social order must be
backed by economic muscle and the military now justify
their power monopoly by pointing out the economic results
of the last few years.

Brazil's industrial growth rates for the 1968–71 period
are presented by official propagandists as a launching platform for an economic miracle. The "economic miracle"
produced by military rule is based on income concentration
in the hands of a few and has a staggering social cost. Very
early on two important decisions were made: to transfer the
main burden of anti-inflationary policies to the wage-earning
sector, whose buying power was reduced, and to cut out
economic deadwood by promoting mergers and industrial

concentration. On the other hand, as some hope had to be given the middle class unable to recycle rapidly, a sort of failproof lottery was put to work for half a year—the stock market. For the urban poor, who represent a direct political threat, bread and circuses were provided by a national sports lottery based on football results.

Dictatorships never have had any trouble making trains run on time, controlling inflation and generally managing the economy. They juggle statistics, build eye-catching monuments and public works. When mistakes are made they have sufficient repressive power to cover them up or to silence the opposition. But there is more to the "Brazilian miracle" than this manipulative capacity common to all dictatorships.

Brazil's model has two striking traits: high profits and the progressive marginalization of 90 per cent of the population. After several years of good statistical growth, the 1970 census results brought a bad surprise to government propagandists. They showed that 32 per cent of those who work in Brazil—which number is less than 45 per cent of the population—earn half the minimum wage and have to survive on 20 U.S. dollars or less a month; 29 per cent earn between twenty and forty dollars and 20 per cent between forty and one hundred dollars. Only 1 per cent of wage earners make more than two hundred dollars a month. These figures, however, did not change the technocrats' plans to concentrate on the 19 per cent of workers who make more than one hundred dollars. The government bought their support and thus assured an expanding consumer market for high- and medium-priced industrial goods. The reasoning is that even if only one in ten Brazilians can buy more than his daily food and a piece of cloth to cover himself, this represents a market of 9.5 million people, more than the population of Sweden. If the market develops rapidly, the concentrated prosperity will eventually drip down to the underprivileged sectors, either through state-guided income distribution or by the industrialists' initiatives to raise their workers' salaries in order to increase the number of buyers. Meanwhile, since the wage squeeze is reducing the market for low-priced goods, such as shoes and cotton cloth, the government subsidizes their export in order to keep the mills running—just as developed nations subsidize farm products to keep agriculture going.

Export subsidies for Brazilian manufactured goods, from plywood to sophisticated machinery, can run as high as 40 or 50 per cent of their domestic price. Subsidies are advantageous to international capitalists. First, by financing exports through inflationary policies the Brazilian government increases its hard currency reserves, which are used partly to repay short-term loans multinational corporations raise in foreign markets to speculate in Brazil. As of 1971, Brazilian reserves were of 1,200 million dollars while its short-term debt was of 1,700 million and more than 30 per cent of export earnings were earmarked to repay foreign loans and interests. Secondly, since the LAFTA (Latin American Free Trade Association) treaty makes it easier for multinational corporations to sell their Brazilian-made products in other Latin American countries, which have lower custom barriers among themselves, than to ship them directly from the U.S. or Europe, the export drive is ideal for them. They profit both from Brazil's write-offs and subsidies and from the importing country's market, which otherwise would probably be closed to them.

Brazil has become a springboard for large corporations interested in Latin America because of its size and the possibilities it offers in neighboring markets. Brazilian technocrats favor the idea of turning the country into a privileged satellite of international capitalism. They hope that this will create new industrial jobs for the better-off part of the marginalized population and that some of the profits made by the Brazilian branches of foreign companies will stay in Brazil, increasing the country's saving capacity.

Although export subsidies are important for some companies, the economy's extremely high profits are maintained by a combination of salary squeezes (see Chapter 5) and stimulation of a middle- and upper-class consumer syndrome. The automobile industry's strategy, for instance, consists in courting the lower-middle-class market by extending credit rather than by reducing prices. It is possible to buy a car in Brazil on a five-year loan. Since its primary market—the privileged classes—has a highly elastic demand, the industry prefers to produce a smaller number of high-priced models than a larger number of lower-priced cars. In this way competition is restricted to a selected market in which style and luxury have the edge instead of low price. The result is that the industry's future is linked to income concentration, a fact that produces such grotesque distortions for an underdeveloped country as advertising campaigns to sell second and third family cars.

Of the many distortions produced by the ruling alliance of foreign capital and native technocrats, perhaps the one that has caused the greatest social stress is the misuse of tax write-offs for investment purposes. Initially the idea behind this scheme was to channel personal and corporate income tax money to industrialization projects in the Northeast, under the supervision of SUDENE, Superintendencia do Desenvolvimento do Nordeste, a government-controlled authority. After the military take-over these tax deductions were so extended that it is now possible to avoid income tax altogether by earmarking money for hotel building, forestry enterprises, cattle ranching in the Amazon, fishing industries, etc.[5] To build an industry in the Northeast one need only put up 12.5 per cent of the capital, the rest being financed by the government often at negative interest rates. As a result the region's many new industries are capital intensive, for it is cheaper to buy automated machinery than to employ people, even at the prevailing starvation wages. Instead of the million new industrial jobs SUDENE had planned to create during its first ten years, only 60,000 new ones were opened, a good percentage of which demand skilled labor that must come from the South. And a greater average investment is needed to open an industrial job in Brazil's Northeast than in the United States.

The enormous extension of tax deductions is yet another consequence of Brazil's dependence. Multinational corporations in need of a market for their luxury goods inspired the government to stimulate conspicuous consumption. A

[5] An analysis of these tax write-offs is found in Thomas G. Sanders, "Making Money: From Animal Game to Stock Market," American University Field Staff Reports, East Coast South America Series, Vol. XIV, No. 4, 1970.

double distortion resulted: the government must rely increasingly on indirect taxes to support itself and the concentrated wealth of the privileged is not used for investment purposes. Indirect taxes, 62.8 per cent of the central government's revenues in 1961, were responsible for 76.7 per cent of its revenues in 1968.[6] This means that official talk about income tax reform and large numbers of new taxpayers since the military take-over is simply another piece of government propaganda. Instead of milking the rich the regime soaks the poor.

As for savings for investment purposes, the 15 per cent to 17 per cent of Brazil's GNP looks pale compared with Japan's 30 per cent—and private investment is only a fraction of this figure. The situation, however, does not affect multinational corporations, which expand by reinvesting earnings and have first call on credit available at local commercial banks. However, it greatly hinders the growth of private Brazilian enterprises, which depend exclusively on national savings for expansion and often for working capital. Governmental responsibility for more than 60 per cent of all investments is again a situation that favors foreign corporations. This money is concentrated in infrastructure public works—roads, dams, communications, etc.—which create a market for the equipment these corporations manufacture in Brazil, or in heavy industries, another large market for heavy equipment.

The end product of these policies is a mongrel economy, born of the intimate association of the state and the foreign corporations. It excludes the possibility of the development of a national bourgeoisie which could fulfill the anti-imperialistic and nation-building functions of its nineteenth-century American and European counterparts. For Brazil's bourgeoisie the choice is either to become a minor partner of international capitalism—living in luxury from its plentiful crumbs—or to disappear.

Wealth concentration creates problems that cannot be dealt with by police repression. The poorest 20 per cent of

6 Inter-American Development Bank, "Social-Economic Progress in Latin America," Ninth Annual Report, Washington, D.C., 1969, p. 74.

the population, with only 4.2 per cent of the national income, is already counted out. But some bones must be thrown to those who have what in Brazil is regarded as a middle-class income.

From 1969 to mid-1971, the stock market was the middle classes' Eldorado as well as a gold mine for the rich. The government took several measures aimed at organizing share trading, which it considered a possible base for "mass capitalism" that could breed widespread support for the system. Share trading, at the same time, provided new resources for company expansion and an expedient way for capitalists to invest out of stagnant industries into dynamic ones. The ever-present tax write-offs were extended to share buyers. Companies were allowed to redress their assets' book value without paying taxes, and many benefits were offered to companies willing to go public. As a consequence investment banks acquired a decisive importance and there was a spectacular bull market. During the first five months of 1971 a speculative frenzy pushed prices sky-high. Some shares rose more than 700 per cent. Two went up 1,100 per cent. The increase in steel-industry shares was 340.3 per cent from January to May, and bank stocks rose 210.5 per cent. Only two shares fell out of a total of four hundred. Taxi drivers, housewives, civil servants, everyone tried to get shark loans to play the market. The SNI (National Information Service) drew preferential lists of military officers to whom government companies were to sell shares at their offering prices, for a few weeks later their value multiplied. People sold their cars, apartments, TV sets, anything to raise cash. Some thirty thousand instant brokers started to knock on doors and peddle financial papers. Prices were boosted or depressed by rumors, crooked deals—called *puxadas* (push-ups)—and more or less reliable "inside" information. One company saw its shares double a few weeks before going bankrupt.

The orgy, though short-lived, didn't end with the crash that most observers predicted. The government couldn't afford the political loss of such a disaster. As 57 per cent of the stock market consisted of shares of state-owned banks and companies which are independent of the market for their capital, official control kept the bottom from falling out quickly. Although prices dropped, many investors had time to pocket their gains and pack off on tours of Europe or the United States to wait for the next government-sponsored bonanza.

Strengthening the upper middle classes and their technocratic friends, favoring multinational corporations, creating tax incentives for mergers, and similar measures are all part of a scheme cynically called "Operation Euthanasia" by the Finance Ministry's young planners.

The basic idea of "Operation Euthanasia" is to waste no money on regions and populations unable to follow the development of the country's more dynamic poles. If the hungry are hard to feed, the illiterate bothersome to employ, let them stay as they are. If the sick are expensive to heal, let them die. If the development of the Northeast and of Minas Geraes' depressed areas calls for extra investments, let these regions go on being exploited by prosperous industrialized São Paulo, where the real government investment effort should be made for quick profits. An example: more money is being sunk just in São Paulo's new subway system than in the industrialization of the Northeast since 1960. In the long run, if social tensions become threatening, technocrats believe they can always devise an emergency program to quiet the crisis area.

The federal budget reflects "Operation Euthanasia." In 1971 only 1.1 per cent of the budget was allocated to public health and 5.1 per cent to education, this last mostly to finance the universities that enroll only 2.3 per cent of the country's students. In contrast 14.3 per cent goes to public works, 13.5 per cent to the Armed Forces. As for internal security figures, they are kept secret.[7]

"Operation Euthanasia" is a Brazilian counterpart of the Vietnamization program—an attempt to co-opt some sectors of society while dooming or intimidating others and keeping power firmly in the hands of those have a stake in capitalism.

The absence of foreign-invasion threats can lead to misinterpretations of the Brazilian political situation. One of these is the "dual power theory" which certain so-called "lib-

[7] *Tribuna da Imprensa*, Rio de Janeiro, October 19, 1971.

eral" scholars from the United States and Europe are fond of promoting.

This "dual power theory" assumes that Brazil is better off under capitalism than under socialism. It sees the present government divided between two forces—a technocratic, modernizing elite that runs the administration and a repulsive, repressive system, allied to the backward interests of the traditional landowners, which is responsible for torture and terrorism. The technocrats are seen as unconnected with the torturer. Their economic performance is praised rather than analyzed. The benefit of the doubt is extended to them when they say they favor a bourgeois democracy but are powerless to bring it about. No explanation is given as to why the torturers' power should be independent of the administration and what are the functional reasons for repression.

Brazil does have a complementary power structure, which, if it suggests duality, is a necessary consequence of the regime's policies and of the country's dependence. In an independent totalitarian nation the dictator heads both the administration and the repressive apparatus. He is free from foreign pressures because his power stems from his control of party and people. He can use external opposition as an instrument to unify public opinion behind the regime. The dictator personifies an ideology capable of mobilizing the masses, and the personal cult he creates is part of nation building because he is presented as the ultimate repository of the country's virtues. He is The Chief, The Leader, The People's Father. He may not personally control all parts of the repressive machine, but nothing is done against his will or to his surprise.

In an independent dictatorship the center of power is not within the country's boundaries but in the capital of the dominant empire. The impression of duality that such a dictatorship gives springs in part from the geographic displacement of the decision-making bureaucracy. In the colony there are really two competing groups, but they obey a single political will. The international community clearly recognizes the situation although in the satellite country it may be masked by proclamations of independence and nationalistic posturings. China and the Soviet Union would never dream of holding to account the occupants of the presidential palaces in Saigon or Brasília for their government's actions, just as the United States does not hold responsible the presidents of Tibet and the Ukraine. Whenever their actions offend a great power the protest is addressed to the power responsible for the satellite.

At most, however, a dependent nation can have a local autocracy, but never a totalitarian regime. The case of Brazil is a good example. The President is the head of the administration and he must balance his acts according to the interests of foreign civilian pressure groups. Normally these groups call for only a limited repression capable of defending their profits. They favor, for instance, outlawing strikes, but feel that heavy-handed repression is bad for business as well as for their nerves. Repeated roadblocks, street shootings, search-and-kill operations are in their opinion too harsh considering the actual threat that revolutionary groups represent to the regime. Their reasons for opposing vast search operations such as those launched after the Swiss ambassador was kidnaped are very objective—they paralyze a large city for several days, causing substantial economic losses. Repressive violence can also lead to revolutionary violence against businessmen, as in the case of Henning Boilensen, a Danish-born industrialist, machine-gunned in São Paulo on April 15, 1971, for financing a military torture center.

The fact that the dominant country's decision center is located in one place does not mean that its political decisions are always marked by unity. In a pluralistic system such as the American, there is a place for conflicting and even contradictory decisions which are reflected in the satellite's internal organization. The most active American pressure groups in Brazil are civilian, linked to the American civilian administration, the embassy, and the State Department. Their goals may not always coincide with those of the invisible power structure, the CIA, and the Defense Department, who are guided by the same security rationale that moves Brazilian military. The CIA and the Pentagon have open lines to Brazilian secret police and the officers in charge of anti-subversive activities. Both tend to reinforce their trainees' power even if occasionally their policies are frowned on by the civilian authorities.

An internal logic based on security needs is essential for an efficient repressive system. Broader economic and social objectives are necessary for a well-run administration. This contradiction leads to an ironic situation. Brazilian presidents come to power because of their military leadership, since they are elected by the barracks. As soon as they take office they are forced to negotiate with civilian groups. The nature of their power becomes "civilized" and, therefore, incomplete and challengeable. The internal-security centers resist restrictions the President may try to impose in compliance with civilian pressures. In the course of time military interests become both political and financial and they are ready to defend them. The result is a deadlocked power struggle, in which the decisive foreign interference is normally also neutralized by the conflicting influences of the American civilian and military authorities. Only threatening crises break the deadlock. Security arguments then prevail both in the satellite and the superpower.

The antagonistic qualities of military leadership needed by a general to become President, on the one hand, and of civilian flexibility he needs to run the country, on the other, explains why Brazilian dictators are progressively more brutal as they emerge from successive crises. Castelo Branco, the first dictator, was a general staff officer who used only the strictly necessary force to implement his policies. Costa e Silva, his successor, was a rednecked trooper far more erratic and given to overreacting to real or imagined threats. Garrastazu Medici, currently in office, supported routine torture when he was Secret Service chief and follows the same line now. His election against a general thought to be nationalistic was a victory for the Pentagon, where he had made friends while head of the Brazilian liaison staff in Washington. He has not disappointed his patrons.

Increasingly repressive presidents helped shape a terrorist state. The security establishment has grown rapidly during the last eight years. There are now 274,000 policemen, of whom 100,000 "benefited" from American training know-how in Brazil itself and 6,858 were trained in the U.S., according to USAID.[8] Their equipment was modernized with American help and their command centralized by the Army. Informers are everywhere, even on the beaches and in the coffeehouses of Rio's affluent suburbs. Their freedom of action is virtually absolute. One of their golden rules is that a Secret Service officer never interferes with a colleague's arrest. The security establishment uses thought control, spying, propaganda manipulation, and plain fear. Every Brazilian is a suspected subversive to the police and a suspected informer to his neighbors. This atmosphere of suspicion is the regime's defensive tool. Torture, searches, unexplained imprisonments, executions, and secret murder are its offensive arms.

The seeming duality between the civilian and military systems is more and more diluted, as repressive officers succeed in choosing the President and their American military allies prevail against the advocates of milder policies in the State Department. Thus Brazil becomes a country covered by fear. No one outside the repressive system—not even the technocrats who make the administration work—can feel secure. Today's most powerful leaders are tomorrow's potential victims.

Reaction, too, devours its children.

[8] "United States Policies and Programs in Brazil," hearings before the Subcommittee on Western Hemisphere Affairs, U. S. Senate, May 4, 5, and 11, 1971, p. 85.

CHAPTER XI

A GRAIN OF MUSTARD SEED

Brazil's liberation will succeed only if we never lose sight of the masses' hidden potential to wage war against a system that will always deny them the right to humanity. The awakening of our revolution will have to be based on a realistic evaluation of the enemy to be conquered as well as on the organized strength of the people.

In 1966, when parliamentary elections offered a possibility of sabotaging from the inside the so-called authoritarian-democratic model, the ESG (Superior War College) tried to establish a lasting political institution, many militants rejected this opportunity, arguing that elections would only rekindle liberal and reformist illusions. While claiming to be Marxist-Leninists, they had not read Lenin's lessons and had forgotten the Bolshevik's participation in a tsarist Duma. They had also failed to learn from the Algerian and Vietnamese experiences of electoral boycotting, which show how hard it is even for strong revolutionary movements battling a foreign invader to keep a police state from herding people to the polls. Seen in perspective this dispute seems futile. A revolutionary movement can use any instrument suited to a tactical situation so long as its strategic goals are always kept in mind.

Making no claim to orthodoxy, I let my intuition about Brazil guide me, and I sided with those who believed we should make the most of every chance to undermine the dictatorship's plans. This purely personal opinion corresponded with the Communist Party analysis but conflicted with AP (Ação Popular) idea of boycott and blank ballots. Then, as now, I thought the masses always tend to follow the line of least resistance and never opt for violent struggle if there are effective legal ways for "the pursuit of happiness," as the American Founding Fathers called social justice. But when the line of least resistance becomes armed struggle they will support it.

My decision to try for election was also influenced by pride, egoism and other less recommendable motives. All popular politicians had been forced into exile or stripped of political rights. They left a void that made the election of a journalist well known for his opposition to the regime quite an easy matter. The temptation to be a congressman—even a castrated one—was difficult to resist for someone brought up in the parliamentary tradition. And, of course, the rather high esteem in which I held myself made me think that I could perform the task of institution-undermining better than most. This opinion, at least, was vindicated by events.

The political model dreamed up by the Superior War College staff is now dead and buried. The dictatorship has proved unable to stabilize an institutional framework capable of drawing the consensual allegiance of the country's middle classes, not to speak of the whole Brazilian people. Forced to rule by terror and to change its own laws every time a crisis occurs, it is an essentially unbalanced regime. This, however, does not mean that its internal contradictions will automatically lead it to self-destruction or that the inevitable quarrels within the only existing political party, the Army, will open possibilities of popular political participation. On the contrary, as social tensions mount, the military moves toward more repressive measures, not more liberal ones. And when the dependent formulas for economic development fail, the tendency will be for a fascist nationalism, not a socialist one.

In 1968, a group of political opportunists, who until recently had been some of the United States' best friends in Brazil, tried to form an "Ample Front" under the leadership of Carlos Lacerda, Rio's right-wing former governor. They put out a platform calling for a return to liberal-democratic rule. They tried an alliance with "Nasserist" and nationalistic military groups. After a few meetings the Front was outlawed and eventually its organizers were shorn of their political rights.

In 1969, the Minister for Internal Affairs, General Albuquerque Lima, tried to unify the nationalistic groups within the Armed Forces. He argued in favor of better income distribution among the country's regions and of some anti-American measures. Fired on the spot, he lingered on the political scene as a presidential possibility. When Costa e Silva died, Albuquerque Lima was said to be supported by most young officers quartered at the strategically based First Army Barracks in Rio. To play safe, he called the New York *Times* correspondent and had him publish a statement to the effect that his nationalism was not directed against foreign investments or the United States. The embassy apparently was not impressed. General Garrastazu Medici, with better pro-American credentials, was chosen. Albuquerque Lima accepted without protest an early retirement and disappeared from politics.

The way the regime coped with these two efforts, which threatened neither the imperialist hold of the economy nor the society's power structure, should be enough to convince socialist forces that there is no salvation within the system. Unfortunately, however, the orthodox Communist Party was not convinced. It now devotes the same energy once employed in searching for a national independent bourgeoisie to the new search for a nationalistic faction in the Armed Forces.

Illusion hunting is a dangerous sport for a country that has little time to lose. The technological gap between the rich and the poor halves of the world is greater today than when the Portuguese, the Spanish, and the British first fired their guns against the natives of their empires, four hundred years ago. The gap widens with alarming speed. The last quarter of this century will undoubtedly decide the sort of world there will be for a long time. The underdeveloped peoples who miss the chance of liberating themselves now will find it difficult later on to catch up to the advanced ones. Even if capitalism disappears by itself—an improbably optimistic idea—a world-wide division of labor will persist, favoring the developed nations. And if capitalism is powerful enough to maintain control of the underdeveloped nations' resources, these nations' chances of ever producing enough to feed, house and educate their populations will be dim in the extreme.

For Brazil the time is now. We can either become India or China. It is in the interest of capitalism that we become India. It is in our interest—and in the long run of mankind— that we become China. We must start at once.

The transformation of our society will have to be imposed on Brazil's privileged classes by force. It will have to be wrested from imperialism through sacrifices we are yet unable to imagine. Even if the American capacity for intervention seems weakened by the Vietnam fiasco and the protests of a youth tired of dying for unworthy causes, the situation can rapidly reverse itself. The United States may form a professional army—and mercenaries never question orders. It can now wage a fearfully destructive war from the skies almost without risking the lives of its pilots. The possibilities for long-distance bombing and scientific warfare can only increase with time. Those who regard the great American empire as paralyzed by internal conflicts and unable to fight for its colonies are spreading illusions that can be dearly paid for. We must face the fact that the task before us is gigantic. It will tax our people to the limit.

Another illusion is to think that chances still exist of reconciling the interests of the people with those of the ruling class. The military dictatorship has slammed shut all doors to a bloodless political evolution. The Chilean model —if it develops into one—is unthinkable in Brazil. Not only do our institutions and political traditions differ widely but Brazil is much too important to the United States to be allowed to drift out of its sphere of influence without violent intervention. On the other hand, it is unrealistic to believe that revolutionary organizations will be able to skip steps and immediately lead an unpoliticized people into a protracted war without adapting their programs to the masses' needs and understanding. To think that in Brazil a revolutionary vanguard of highly ideologicized supermen can make the revolution *for* the people instead of *with* the people is suicidal elitist nonsense.

After three years of intermittent armed strife, Brazil's revolutionary movements are, in 1971, at their lowest ebb. Urban guerrillas have been unable to shake the dictatorship. The groups are divided, small, powerless. They failed to mobilize the masses and even to capitalize on the sympathy produced by some of their actions. No political structures capable of sustained development were formed. Repression has terrorized the middle classes and cut out the help some of its sectors gave to guerrilla fighters. Counterpropaganda and lack of serious political work turned popular opinion against the revolutionaries. The price paid for the experience was more than just giving the regime time to prepare its defenses: many of the best revolutionary leaders were killed; thousands were arrested or went into exile.

The defeats urban guerrillas suffered are the result of bad political analysis. When Marighela started to act he did not want to set up a new revolutionary model or to conquer power with a handful of determined men. He was not a putschist but an impatient man entangled in a castrating bureaucracy. He had been a militant member of the Communist Party too long not to realize that without mass organizing he couldn't go far. What he tried to do was to short-circuit paralyzing internal discussions and demonstrate that the dictatorship was not invulnerable, that it could and should be attacked. He hoped this demonstration would split the Communist Party and provide him with sufficient political authority to start a revolutionary front made up of militants of many different origins. In such a front the armed activities of urban guerrillas were to be like the small, visible part of an iceberg. Most militants would devote themselves to the political work necessary to anchor the struggle on firmer bases. Tactical mistakes, underestimation of repressive forces and Marighela's early death (November 4, 1969) wrecked this plan.

Once the urban guerrilla was launched it monopolized Marighela's attention. As there were not enough militants to divert to long-term political work his ALN (Ação Libertadora Nacional) had to recruit among already "conscientized" members from other political organizations or from student movements. Lack of firm popular bases, as well as the almost immediate appearance of other guerrilla groups, hindered the build-up of the revolutionary front. The result was that each group sought to overstate its position, looking rather for the fine theoretical points that give them a separate identity than for the broad area of agreement all had in common. This hair-splitting delayed unification until Marighela's death. Since then the havoc spread by repression slowed it up and progress has been half-hearted. So much has already been lost that what is needed is a completely new strategy.

Two main factors accounted for the dictatorship's victories: the class origins of urban guerrilla fighters and the unsuspected efficiency of torture as an information-gathering method. Most urban guerrilla groups came from the middle class: students, young professionals, ex-sergeants and officers, white-collar workers. This class origin forced the organizations to establish their operative bases on enemy territory—the apartments and houses of the big cities—for the guerrillas could easily be spotted in the shantytowns and suburbs where the working class lives. This proved to be a disastrous security mistake. The police soon established a control system through doormen and watchmen. On top of this the revolutionaries more easily fell victim to informers, for they could not count on the political solidarity of the class among which they lived. They became, at the same time, further isolated from the masses. Instead of fishes in the sea of the people they were foxes on an open field, with the hounds close to their heels.

The efficiency of torture was also partly a consequence of bad organizing and superficial political training. Had the guerrilla cells been well sealed off from one another the chain reactions provoked by the arrest of some militants could not have happened. In one case—the arrest of a student after a bank holdup in Rio de Janeiro—a single prisoner led to the discovery of more than fifty apartments and houses used by his group, the destruction of the PCBR, Brazilian Revolutionary Communist Party, in Rio and the jailing of the party's entire leadership.

Had the political persuasion of some arrested militants been more deeply rooted they would not have spilled all the facts they knew, and the number willing to renounce publicly their revolutionary commitments in exchange for freedom or a light sentence would have been far smaller. Bad political training results from the security precautions urban guerrillas must take in order to survive. Repression makes it difficult to approach possible recruits in a step-by-step manner. Discussion meetings, semi-open debates, study groups are extremely risky to organize. A recruit must be accepted as already politically formed when he is invited to join a group. After he joins there is only one job—direct armed action, for the organizations have very few legal activities. Quickly he is forced underground, into a totally clandestine life that offers little opportunity for study and formative discussions. The time gap between political awareness and clandestinity is often brief. In the space of a few months a student discovers our country's realities, reacts against them, takes part in student demonstrations, is noticed simultaneously by revolutionary groups and the secret police, joins the guerrillas, takes part in illegal actions and is arrested or forced into exile. It is only in prison or abroad that he has a real chance to re-examine his commitment and study its ideological implications. No wonder then that some reverse their decisions and try to save their skins by offering their services to the government. If Brazilian conditions were not so sharply drawn in black and white, oppressors against oppressed, it is probable that the number of desertions would be greater. Doubt would take its toll. Conditions being what they are, only those who do not care to see could doubt about which side stands for justice and independence. If one is sure of the justice of one's cause desertion is a difficult choice to live with.

Security needs are also partly to blame for the difficulties guerrilla organizations face in forming working class cells. Political work through the police-controlled trade unions is almost impossible. Parallel structures and communication channels are unsafe and take a long time to organize. Contacts between workers and the organizations have to be slow and wrapped in all sorts of precautions. Recruiting activities in the *favelas* and low-priced housing areas are also difficult, hampered as they are by security measures and the militants' class origins. And so we fall in a vicious circle of movements

unable to develop for lack of a social base, and social bases
that cannot be formed owing to security.

Most revolutionary organizations have spotted and analyzed these faults. Some have soft-pedaled their activism in
order to reform their strategy, think up new tactics and se-
riously look into establishing a revolutionary front of organizations that could be the core of a larger liberation front.
Others, while going through the formal motions of internal
discussions and self-criticism, refuse to see their errors. They
radicalize their rhetoric and insist on the same methods.
Some of their militants go as far as to think that to change
the course of action is to betray their fallen comrades and
the cause of the revolution. They don't see that the worst
betrayal is to fail to lead the revolution to victory. Organizations that dodge reality are doomed and will pass into Brazilian history as a bloody footnote.

Clichés are comfortable mental shields to protect our
inability to reason. Some militants try to explain the many
defeats our revolutionary movement suffered by saying that
the way to progress is by "taking two steps forward and one
backward" or that we are in a "phase in which forces are
accumulated." If a correct strategy is not devised all our
steps will be backward and there will never be enough accumulated forces to strike the enemy. It is obvious that urban
guerrillas will exist as long as the dictatorship survives. They
are the answer of a radicalized and hot-blooded youth to a
situation of intolerable oppression. But, spectacular as their
actions may be, they will not alter the balance of power within
our society. On the contrary, if they don't join larger popular
forces and help mobilize them, they may have the reverse
effect of strengthening the influence of the most repressive
military groups. As a consequence political life could become
limited to a contest between the small revolutionary armed
groups and the government's large counter-revolutionary
army. The people can only be a spectator of such a struggle,
with no possibility of taking part in it or influencing its outcome.

Brazil's revolution can only develop if it broadens its
political and social basis. It is essential, as a first step, to convince most of the orthodox Communist Party, still the best-

organized part of the country's socialist forces, of the need to take the only alternative the regime has left open—armed struggle. It is equally important to enroll in this struggle the young Catholic militants, with their habits of discipline, logistical support, and acceptance by the masses. In a second phase some sectors that are now, through fear or opportunism, more inclined to side with the regime must be mobilized. They are the lower-middle-class sectors, the small shopkeepers, the small landowners, civil servants, professional people, even the influence-peddling chieftains of the underdeveloped interior. They have no particular stake in an income-concentrating system and no fundamental quarrel with a socializing program. And all this effort must lead toward the organization of a revolutionary mass party that will have to conduct the armed phase of the liberation process.

Revolutionaries must be flexible and non-sectarian in order to build a broad political front. They must learn to detect and exploit the most painfully felt local contradictions between the people and the regime. Plans must be adapted to the people's level of political perception, which only slowly can be broadened. Respect for the masses must be a permanent guideline in action, not an exercise in rhetoric.

The revolutionary front must include a plurality of opinions with the right to express themselves and with influence on the working out of general policies. Its decision-making process must be one of centralized democracy so that the political and military aspects of the struggle can be properly guided. This, however, must not transform democratic consultation of militant cells in a formal exercise as is so often the case in bureaucratized parties. The militants' opinions must really be taken into account. The front's program must voice the minimum basic policies around which the widest possible consensus can be reached.

A program for a liberation front will galvanize the energies of each militant only if he recognizes in it the result of his own work and thoughts, the expression of his hopes and his vision of a world to be built. If, on the contrary, such a program is the brainchild of a group and is imposed by a leadership, it will fail to trigger the dedication and selflessness of which revolutions are made.

The time of man flows faster than the time of history. We are always impatient to live our dreams to their final results. But we now face a task that has only begun, a task that may consume more time than we are ready to surrender, but a task we cannot hasten. If we refuse to follow its rhythm, if we try to force its natural pace too much, we may slow its maturing and perhaps never accomplish it.

Liberation is "like a grain of mustard seed, which, when it is sown in the earth, is less than all the seeds that be in the earth. But when it is sown, it groweth up, and becometh greater than all herbs, and shooteth out great branches; so that the fowls of the air may lodge under the shadow of it."

Cornille, May 1971
Paris, November 1971

INDEX